The Ultimate Explanation

Imagine, if you will, an overall scheme that explains a new fourth dimension, gravity, space, time, the shape of the universe and even the existence of a Greater Intelligence.

A scheme that identifies the mind, explains what it is, how the universe came about, its purpose and our purpose within it, and what happens to us when we die.

A scheme that describes what we are and what it's all about without the use of religion or myth.

That, no matter how imaginative, takes you on a voyage of discovery based on nothing but pure logic and reason.

By the vehicle-of-communication within these humble pages, such a voyage of discovery now lies before you.

A REMARKABLE NEW THEORY

The Ultimate Explanation

for the Thinking Layman

The meaning of life,
a fourth dimension,
space, time, gravity, the
shape and purpose of the universe,
and the mind of a Greater Intelligence

Robert Norfolk

Ranwaters

First published in 1994
by Ranwaters
31 Hall plain, Gt. Yarmouth,
Norfolk. NR30 2QD

British Library Cataloguing-in-Publication Data.
A catalogue record for this book is available from the British
Library.

ISBN: 0-9523508-0-7

Printed by Page Bros, Norwich
Cover photography & design by Michael Clifford
© Michael Clifford1994
Cover-typeset by David Doddington

Dedications

"Mum, is Dad dead?"
"No dear, he's writing a book."

To Suzanne for her infinite patience, and our Sons,
Alexander and Ross.

Mum, Dad, Roger and Nick for their unfailing support.

Acknowledgements

Caithness Glass Ltd, Perth, for their very kind permission
to use the "Encounter" paperweight, designed for Caithness
Glass Ltd by Colin Terris.

CONTENTS

INTRODUCTION

Angle of approach

There is no one that understands a concept better than the originator. To then communicate that concept by the written word is something that requires great skill, a skill quite separate from that required to originate the concept in the first place. My best efforts for such an exercise are driven by perpetually 'craning my neck' to view from the readers perspective, an effort that will often result in a multiangled approach.

Put another way (!) To expect an onlooker to identify an etching, concealed beneath a brass rubber's tracing paper, by just one broad stroke of a crayon, is unreasonable indeed. Yet the man doing the brass rubbing, having seen the etching in its full glory before laying on the tracing paper, may consider one stroke sufficient. The onlooker will demand many strokes from varying angles before a full appreciation of what lies beneath becomes apparent, and quite rightly so.

I try to bear this in mind. And with your mind, please, I ask, lay it open and judge only at the end.

Gender

My apologies to women readers. I have had to plump for either He or She throughout and at the flip of a coin I have gone for He. I intend to infer no preference.

Structure of approach

How tempting it would be to tantalisingly "drip-feed" each element of the **true nature of things**. Slowly pulling back the magicians cloak to reveal corner by corner something

1

so obvious that much of it has never been seen before. But that is not what I'm about. Communication is the name of my game and there is nothing that frustrates communication more than having to finish reading a complete section before the general idea is imparted. Great wads of text designed to present an angle, concept or general idea that could just as easily be summarised at the beginning by way of an overview. Certainly, the main body of the text is needed to describe, justify and explore the idea but it's nice to know what the idea is that you are exploring.

To this end, an overview of each part of the book will be presented at its start. An overview with which I shall probably be risking the initial accusation of sounding fantastic. An 'up-front map' that tells the reader where it is I am trying to take him before we start off, albeit a map which is only general. This will be followed by the main body of text in the form of logic, reason and justification behind the embodied concept. Finally, I shall quite often provide a third swipe of the 'credit card of explanation', in that mental 'check-out machine of understanding', in the form of a summary or recap.

What the book is about

Broadly; this is the first of four books all of which will disclose a theory designed to unify all of creation and all phenomena within it. This first book is the "base case" which describes the universe at large. It presents a new theory on life, the Universe and the mind of a Creator, with twelve years of formulation behind it. It is qualitative and highly philosophical with very little maths. It will be explicitly described by use of fantastic journeys, thought experiments, analogies and logical arguments that, amongst other things, endorses the existence of an ether, dispenses with time as a dimension, describes a new fourth dimension and disqualifies space as being empty.

Introduction

It places all this into a new closed, four dimensional, expanding model of the universe, which becomes apparent as a three dimensional infinity (stretching on forever) with no edge and a centre that passes through every point within. This *apparently* infinite shape will then be seen to be finite (*not* stretching on forever), in reality, when the fourth dimension is thoroughly explored and understood within these pages. The book will demonstrate how this model gives rise to the phenomenon we call "gravity" along with an explanation as to how a new four dimensional "steady state universe" manifests itself in such a model, and without the need for the continual creation of matter. None of which, surprising as it may seem, is in conflict with Einstein's "General Relativity" or any other existing or future theories. It will be seen to run in parallel with them by being no more than a different description of the same reality but with the advantage of being further reaching and unified across all the fronts of the reality that it seeks to describe.

All of this is set against a background of what existence really is. Making clear the answer to the questions of what we are, where we are and what our purpose is, along with the '*how*' and more importantly the '*why*' of the universe's existence as a whole. It involves the true meaning of 'mind' and the concept of pure intelligence, detailing how the true nature of existence leads to the world and universe as we experience / perceive it.

It charters unexplored waters by starting from base and running up to where other theories start from, thereby leaving them intact. For example; it doesn't describe what we *call* matter by quantifying, at great length, how it manifests itself. Instead it offers an explanation as to what matter actually *is*, where it comes from and why it bothers to exist in the first place. This then leads to an explanation of the gravity it exhibits as a result of existing.

3

The Why and the How

There are two main elements to the book which should appeal to three sets of reader. There is the metaphysical which describes the true nature of existence: this is a philosophy that explains what exactly existence is, what we are, where we are; the purpose behind it all. In other words; the *why* of all creation. Then there is the physical aspect which is a description of the mechanics behind it all: the push and pull; the "what you see is what you get"; the "if it's heavy then you can't lift it": gravity, space, time, the shape of the universe, a new fourth dimension; the manifestation of physical phenomena within our universe. The *how* of all creation.

The three sets of reader to which these two elements will appeal are of course those two groups each of which is separately interested in one of the elements, and the final group, interested in both. To the group only interested in the physical, please do not allow the metaphysical aspect of part one to put you off. It can be disengaged from the 'how' of the universe, leaving it to stand in its own right.

Other books

This book can only brush the surface. It is the **Base Case** against which the others will follow, forming a continuation of this theory. **Book two** will cover movement in the universe by revealing things like the true nature of light, inertia and much more. **The third** will cover the subatomic world and the unification of the four forces, while **the fourth** will look at the human side of the mind of a Creator: our behaviour, life after death and what constitutes the structure of its mind (also briefly touched upon in this book).

Present thinking

From the above overview to the entire book, it can be seen where it is we are heading. But the question has first to be asked; where is it we have been? Our official custodians of knowledge (Universities, research institutes etc. throughout the world) have given us their ideas and explanations which are to be greatly admired having enabled technology to reach its present level. Their research has lead to incredible feats of human achievement such as putting people into space and splitting the atom.

These custodians of knowledge have provided the development of all aspects of science including Physics, Astrology and Mathematics to name but a few. We have names like Galileo, Newton, Einstein and now Stephen Hawking. As a result we have some very powerful tools that enable the exploration of the world and universe that surrounds us. Sadly, what we don't yet have is a standalone explanation that provides a unified structure which accounts for *all* phenomena, encompassing things like the shape of the universe, the absolute origin of matter and the reason behind the creation of our universe as a whole. Or indeed the amalgamation between the reason for all creation, as described in terms of a Greater Being, and the observations of science. These questions are of course under the close scrutiny of our institutional think tanks (as well as that of the present day **Thinking Layman**). It is the provision of such a single unified theory that this book, and others in the series, seeks to supply.

Certainly, our institutes have some ingenious models that can enable them to perform their close scrutiny of reality to good effect. Quite often the reasoning behind these models would be that there is indeed something there that needs to be modelled, a "something" which might, for instance, be given the name of an "atom". Experiments would indicate certain things about it and give a good idea as to where it hangs out. From all this a picture of what the thing might look like can be constructed with various terminology and numbers applied to its component parts in order to describe what experiments and calculations have indicated. But we still don't know what the thing *really* is (what I call its **true nature**). So, the construction that has been formulated is what is called a "model". A model of reality. What reality is, our institutions know not and this they accept.

These models, and subsequent theories, are therefore based on assumptions. Assumptions that hang in mid-air, no one really knowing what supports them. Now, I'm not saying they are wrong. They must be first class. After all they have enabled some stunningly accurate quantification of phenomena from that level up. But because they are good does not mean we should confuse them with being the ultimate explanation.

Magnetism is a good example of this; we have a model which includes magnetic fluxes from which we have rules such as "opposite poles attract" but no one knows what these lines of flux are made of, apart from to give them a name. Then we have gravity in the form of Einstein's theory of General Relativity: brilliant. A work of inspiration and pure genius but we don't know what it is that conveys gravity other than being due to the warping of space. What is space? Answer: nothing. A vacuum, or at least very nearly. How, therefore can nothing warp? Then we have force carriers called gravitons which pass through space between massive objects to convey the force of gravitational attraction. But these have not as yet been found. We clearly have not got to the bottom of things yet which, in itself, keeps our research institutes gainfully employed.

Further, magnetism doesn't fit with gravity in that gravity cannot be explained by magnetism and vice versa which also suggests that we have not got to the bottom of things. Why should they fit, you might argue, they are separate phenomena. Quite so but for both to be part of the same **overall scheme of things** they must each be driven by the same thing at some lower level that then manifests itself as two separate phenomena at the higher level at which we see them i.e. gravity and magnetism. Not unreasonable you might reply. That being the case, this lower level must be such that *all* phenomena converge to present themselves as a **grand unified theory**. It could hardly be called unified if it could not be equally applied to all phenomena by way of an explanation. The official appointees of social knowledge are intelligent people and by knowing of the potential existence of such a theory, are striving for its attainment. (As they strive, so too, the thinking layman's imagination comes alive).

To return to the model of the atom. We know that the electron is attracted to the nucleus because "opposite charges attract". In this respect the electron has a negative charge and the nucleus has a net positive charge. But what is a charge? No one knows. This underlines the nature of a **constraint**. A constraint that goes to make a model just that; a model and not reality. If we knew all there is to know about a model it would not be a model. It would be reality itself. And so the questions go on through all walks of research.

This mid-air level of knowledge, from which all our theories emanate, is what I call **the plinth of knowledge** and the purpose of this book is to explain what I see as being under that plinth in the form of a single support structure. In fact, I intend to take the reader so far under that plinth, in this and subsequent books in this series, that we will finally *descend down to meet with the* **top** of existing theories, all of which I will leave intact because, as I will explain in part one, all models are viable and correct. A closed loop in other words. A closed loop formed by a new fourth dimension with existing knowledge as its start and finish point and common sense, logic and reason as its boundaries.

The Ultimate Explanation

So there it is. We have some very powerful 'torches', designed and built by our officially appointed 'thinking institutes', enabling us to scan around in the twilight and discover more about our surroundings. But the dim twilight that bathes all we discover is hither to unexplained by way of a single theory. A single theory that would switch on the 'lamp of realisation' to illuminate all things. (The fourth dimension described in this book, leads directly to the light switch - you only need to switch it on).

****

PRELUDE

After the introduction, this book consists of five parts. Part one is predominantly metaphysical in that it is designed to explain the true nature of existence. This it will do by imparting the general concept of there being two levels of existence. It will be seen as the most abstract aspect of the theory, being presented as a preamble to the remainder of the book and as such should not be taken as being typical of the whole book. However, this metaphysical aspect will very much stand in its own right in the final part (part five) as we look more deeply into the mind of a Greater Intelligence.

The remaining parts (two to four) are very much less abstract, comprising more of the physical aspects of the universe by describing the conventionally accepted three dimensions, revealing a new fourth dimension, defining space, time, gravity and much more all by way of this, a single theory that reveals their true nature and answers long standing questions. Having said this, the "true nature of existence" (the metaphysical aspect of two levels of existence) will remain as the backdrop throughout to continually provide the 'why' behind the 'how'. This will then serve to reveal more of the intricate nature of existence than can possibly be described in part one alone.

It has to be said, that the more physical issues, described in parts two to four, do not depend on the concept described in part one; the true nature of existence. They can be disengaged, leaving a tangible description of *how* the physical universe works, but at the cost of being left with no reason *why*.

Always, it will be seen that to know why is then to realise how.

PART 1

EXISTENCE

There are two levels of existence. **First level existence** and **second level existence**. First level existence is pure intelligence of which our minds form part. Second level existence is how the first level of existence appears to us as part of that existence. Both levels of existence are the same thing. I give them different names so as to highlight the two different ways that this same thing can be viewed. Figure one gives an overview of this concept that can be referred to throughout the rest of the book as its meaning becomes clearer.

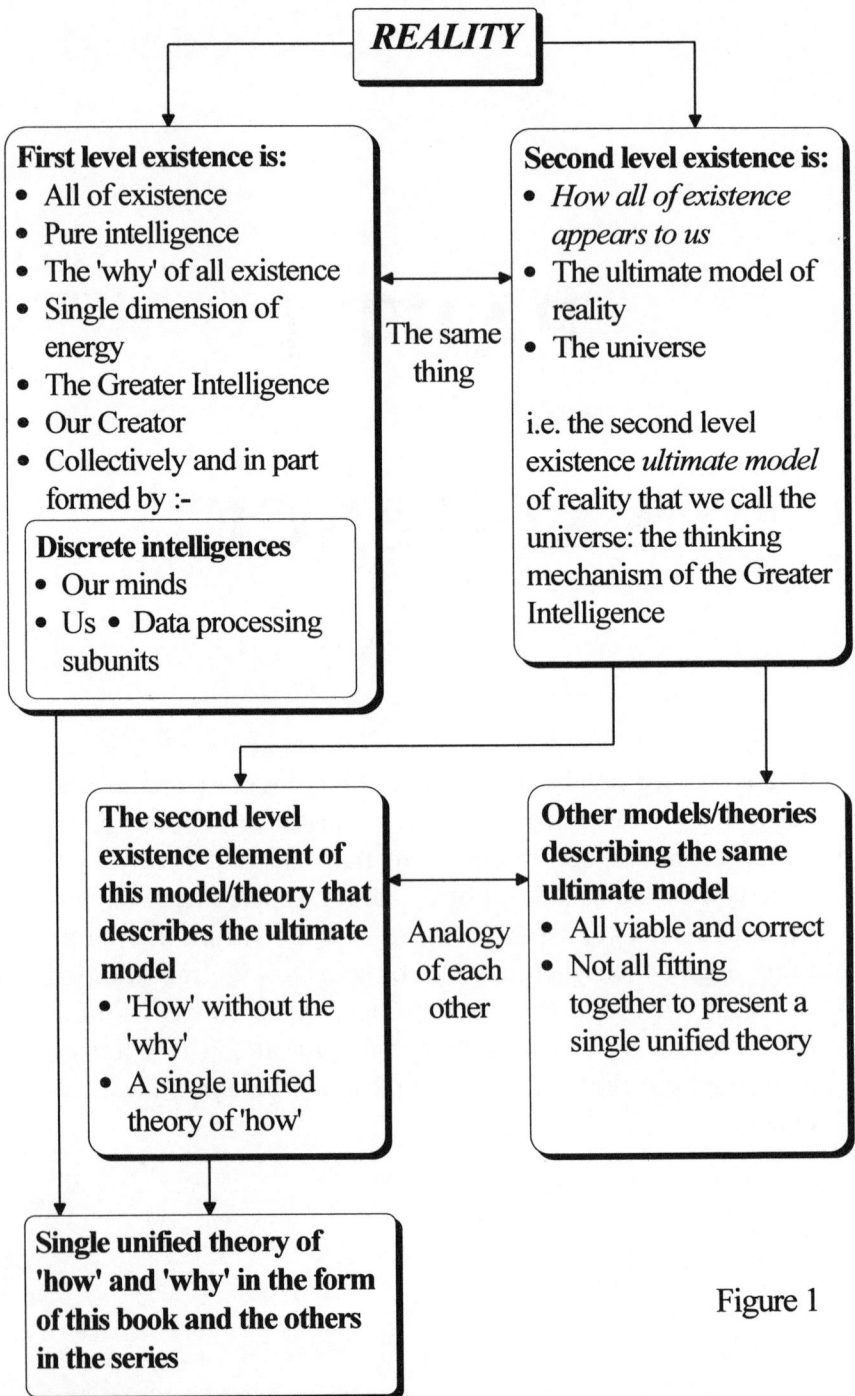

REALITY

First level existence is:
- All of existence
- Pure intelligence
- The 'why' of all existence
- Single dimension of energy
- The Greater Intelligence
- Our Creator
- Collectively and in part formed by :-

Discrete intelligences
- Our minds
- Us • Data processing subunits

The same thing

Second level existence is:
- *How all of existence appears to us*
- The ultimate model of reality
- The universe

i.e. the second level existence *ultimate model* of reality that we call the universe: the thinking mechanism of the Greater Intelligence

The second level existence element of this model/theory that describes the ultimate model
- 'How' without the 'why'
- A single unified theory of 'how'

Analogy of each other

Other models/theories describing the same ultimate model
- All viable and correct
- Not all fitting together to present a single unified theory

Single unified theory of 'how' and 'why' in the form of this book and the others in the series

Figure 1

CHAPTER 1
FIRST AND SECOND LEVEL
EXISTENCE

Really, existence is all there is, full stop. There is not two levels of it, just one which is pure intelligence. I term this as **first level existence**. But this absolute form of intellectual existence is not one that we realise. Unfortunately we have become convinced beyond question of what I call the **second level existence,** which is the universe as it *appears* to be: purely physical. Everything we see, touch, hear, smell and taste is computed in the mind as being the manifestation of physical phenomena experienced as a direct result of interfacing with the universe that surrounds us. The particular part of the universe to which I refer as interfacing with, is obviously our immediate environment within the world that we live. If our society lived on other planets or anywhere, for that matter, in the universe, the term "interfacing with the universe" would equally apply to the immediate universe that impacts with us at those locations.

But when we say "computed in the mind," what do we mean by "mind." It is central to the exercise of figuring out what is happening to the body to which it is connected. After all, it is to this particular piece of kit that all our senses report and as such the mind must be the prime suspect for convincing us that the universe is what it appears to be. So before we can conclude what form the universe really takes we must fully appreciate what we mean by the word "mind."

Mind

Question: how can the physical universe not exist? Response: how do we know that it does?

When you touch a table top with your finger you can feel it, therefore it must physically exist. But how do you know you are touching it? Information travels to your brain to tell you as much. It must therefore be the input to your brain that tells you, not your finger. You can also see it but that is also via inputs to your brain, as indeed if you could smell, taste or hear it. All our senses are inputs to our brains. Whip out your brain, stick it in a tank of water and feed it with the same data and it would still think it was touching the table. Feed it with every piece of data relevant to your previous stance at the said item of furniture and who is to say that the brain, still floating in water, would not be convinced that it was touching and admiring the fine carpentry with which such a beautiful, solid, late eighteenth century, show piece of a table has been produced.

Thought Experiment

Now, many will take my train of thought and see what I mean by it. Some will argue that it is not physically possible to simulate all the necessary inputs to a brain and that it would hurt to remove it in the first place. Sure enough. So, for that second group: PLEASE DO NOT TRY THIS AT HOME! To the first group I ask that you do not consider the following as an offence to your intelligence but, what I have described is an **ideal experiment** in which all the practicalities and real-world-constraints have been removed in order to establish the essence of the logic behind the concept. This is what Einstein referred to as a **thought experiment**. Only able to be performed in one's brain (be it in a tank of water or still recovering from the night before). He used them repeatedly whilst considering the subtleties of Relativity. His famous lift experiment, for instance. He

14

imagined a lift that fell towards earth for as long as he cared to ponder the effects of inertia, which a group of people that were born and raised inside, would discover. It just "ain't possible" but it provided just those aspects of reality that Einstein required to consider.

Touching with the mind

To return to the point in question, what I am saying is that we do not really know for a fact that the universe, that surrounds us, is actually there at all. To know within our own minds, for absolute certainty, that there is something out there that our finger is touching, we really need to reach out and touch it with the very thing that decides whether it is physical or not; our minds.

An excellent analogy for this is to think of a diver in a one-man submarine exploring the depths of the ocean with remote control arms on the outside of his craft. He gropes inside the wreckage as gently as he can to try and find the lost treasure hidden within its hold. The powerful yet highly dextrous hydraulically driven arms 'feel' gently inside the dark hole in which the diver knows the chest to be. His drawings and research have told him its size and shape and right now the proximity sensors on the tips of the arms are outlining just such a shape on his onboard computer screen.

But, the question is this. Having located the booty, does he now grip and remove it, forcing the hole in the side of the hull that much larger to accommodate its passage. By such an extraction he knows he will destroy the entire vessel with no hope of a second chance. So it has *got* to be the chest and not some antediluvian toilet cistern of similar shape and location within the vessel. He shines the bright halogen lamps as best he can into the hold and squints through the thick glass in the port hole but all he can make out is what could be the concave lid of a treasure chest or equally the top of a "Burlington Valveless." The frustration of it all. See next weeks thrilling episode of ....

I digress. The point is this. Despite all the sophisticated feed back he is receiving as the 'brain' of such a craft, he can only truly know what he has in his grip by getting out of the submarine to go and touch and see the thing for himself, within the hold of the sunken vessel. I could imagine words to that effect going through his mind, with a few kindly nautical terms thrown in.

For those with a passion for a good story, the diver was known as "Rip'em Wesley" and successfully removed the chest to reveal untold wealth with which he went on to become Secretary for internal affairs at Chichester Village Ponds Dredging Society.

"Rip'em" was unable to leave the submarine because he had no diving suit. Likewise, we are unable to reach out with our minds to confirm what our senses are telling us. To return to the original question and response: how can the physical universe not exist? Response: how do we know that it does? The answer to the response is quite simply that we don't. We assume that it does because we have no knowledge of any other system. A system that would otherwise describe and support a universe that does not physically exist.

A model of reality

Now, I'm not suggesting that the universe is made up of our brains floating in a large tank of water, connected together by wires that enable us to think we are communicating with each other by way of conventional conversation. Or indeed that these bobbing-brains are also connected to machines that simulate every detail of sensory information required as inputs or indeed; outputs, to produce the sensation of normal every day living and activity. No. What I am suggesting is much more absurd than that. Absurd only because it is nothing more than common sense, as we shall see.

Besides, there are questions that would need to be asked of this 'tank of brains' situation that would show it to be riddled with constraints. Who built the machines and who maintains them for instance? Or; for what reason should our existence take this form, and, more importantly, if the machines existed in the physical sense then the true nature of existence would have to include this physical form and it is a universe in the physical form that I am questioning.

This Brains-in-a-tank-of-water scenario is one that I know you will not take seriously and neither should you. So why am I identifying its short falls at such length? The reason is this. The Brains-in-a-tank-of-water set-up demonstrates what is meant by a **model**. In this case, a model of existence. It nicely presents what could be the facts and delivers them in just the way I intend them to be appreciated. But it is riddled with constraints that show it not to be true reality and it is constraints that make a model just that; a model. If the constraints were not there then it would be because we have no problems with it and as such we would have to conclude it to be reality. Given that the constraints do exist ("who maintains the machines" for instance) we know it is not reality but it would be a pity to throw it out for that reason alone. It satisfactorily presents certain aspects of reality and for that reason I would like to keep it. Our research institutes have cupboards full to the brim with such models.

Second level existence

The above deliberations as to what makes a model is not just an aside. It is vitally important to fully appreciate what a model is and why it should be considered as such for the following simple reason. The entire universe that we perceive as surrounding us, is a model. A model that describes true reality in just the same way that the Brains-in-a-tank-of-water model describes certain aspects of reality. And just as the Brains-in-a-tank scenario is a model because it has constraints, I will describe the constraints that make the perceived physical universe the ultimate model of reality and not reality itself. This Ultimate model of reality is **second level existence** and is quite simply how the universe *appears* to us to be. Obviously, the justification and logic for this seemingly outrageous statement is to follow but for now I am afraid we must first return to our Brains-in-a-tank scenario.

The constraints of a model

Yes, there they are, bless them. A collection of brains floating in a tank of water all wired up as if each personality, locked within his bobbing brain, is living a normal life. Quite a picture and one that we have decided is very far removed from reality by virtue of its constraints but now let us explore just how far it is removed.

This is best done by focusing in on the brain and the best focusing tool to change blur to vision in this respect is to ask one key question: is the brain also the mind? That is: are they one and the same? Answer: no. The reason: why should they be?

To explain this we can start with the fact that all five of our senses feed into the brain and we have discussed a model whereby those inputs could be simulated such that the occupants of the brains would not realise that they were not in the physical world at all. We have also uncovered the constraints of this model, constraints that go to make it an unworkable representation of the **true-nature-of-reality**. But those constraints are driven by the fact that the buoyant brains are considered necessary to support the thinking, reasoning personality. A personality that takes the form of human intelligence which forms the occupant of each brain.

This constraint evaporates if we simply advance the logic applied to the simulation of the inputs to our 'water bound brains' and consider the situation if we were to realise that the brain is also a **pseudo physical manifestation**. By which I mean, there is no more reason to consider the brain as existing in the physical sense than the fine solid-oak table that might supposedly be sitting at the end of our finger when trying to convince ourselves of its physical existence by the sense of touch. The question then arises; if all five senses feed into the brain, and the brain does not physically exist, into what do they feed? Answer: the mind.

First level existence

This opens up a whole new ball-game. This suggests that all there is to existence is mind and what it is that constitutes the mind is a question for which we have always had the answer. In fact, by being able to ponder the answer to this question, we provide it before finishing its consideration: the mind is constituted by Intelligence. Therefore existence must be pure intelligence. We will see that this is not a 'model' because it has no constraints and therefore true reality. Reality which I call **first level existence** which is all of existence in the form of pure intelligence.

Naturally I do not consider the foregoing argument to be in any way conclusive in its own right. It requires justification and analysis which shall be provided in the balance of this book. I shall be describing every detail: what it is made of, where it is, what it looks like, how it works and more. All I ask for now is that you regard it as nothing more than a tangible, although apparently fantastic, suggestion. Let me plant a seed for I intend that you enjoy its growth.

The Greater Intelligence

To provide germination for this seed let me suggest this. That all of intelligence is a **collective intelligence**. One and the same, of which we as individuals form part. We all see the same universe, we all observe the same phenomena and we are all able to communicate with each other because we are part of the same system. We are each separate sub-units of one **Greater Intelligence** which we collectively help to form. Our purpose within such a system is clear cut but before dwelling on such profound issues, by way of reason and common sense, let us return to the subject of the so called physical universe and decide what is meant by the term "physical" in the context of what we now perceive as "mind".

CHAPTER 2
THE PHYSICAL UNIVERSE

"Physical" is only a name

Now that a brief introduction to the true nature of mind has been covered, I can reveal my true colours and tell you, contrary to what you might otherwise think, I completely agree that ultimately our universe is of course physical. How can it be anything else? How indeed? In fact it can be anything we like. I prefer it to be a pink elephant myself. It matters not, as long as what I see as being a "pink elephant" is exactly what you see as being the "physical universe". We are both talking about the same thing but referring to it by different names, and what's in a name? If a statement goes as follows: "the effect of receiving inputs to our minds is as a result of interfacing with the *physical universe,*" then who am I to disagree? The resulting interface must be due to a phenomena of some description and if someone else cares to refer to it as "interfacing with the *physical universe*" then all he has done is given it a name with which I am happy to go along with.

"Physical" has no meaning

That is, if we care to agree that the universe we perceive is what we call *physically existing* then I must concede that what I am experiencing is something called physical existence. But this does not mean that anyone understands what the true nature of existence is, only that we choose to refer to it by the same name as is generally adopted by others: "physical". Just as it is not known what a *charge* truly is (that maintains the atoms structure) other than to give it a name and apply certain rules to it.

Put another way: if everyone in the world agrees to call a certain colour by the name "red" and an alien happens by, to whom we describe that colour as being "red," he could not possibly consider us to be wrong. If we decide "red" is the particular squawky noise we want to come from the hole in the front of that round thing at the top of our bodies in reference to a certain colour each time it is produced, how could the alien possibly deny us that privilege. Despite having a different noise for it himself, we would both be talking about the same thing and each would be equally correct in calling it by whatever name he liked. Then again, we could always see this as an affront to our culture and go to war over it. Another job for Rip'em Wesley perhaps. Defender of human culture and colour charts.

Rip'em Wesley aside, the point in question is that neither the alien nor ourselves would be in contention as to what is being referred to when we make the sound "red". However, what has not, in any way, entered the conversation is the subject of what exactly constitutes this phenomena we call "red". It is simply not necessary. We hold aloft the card with that colour on it, make a certain noise and Albert the alien gets the-drift-of-things allowing our two alien cultures to start the bond of communication, the next step of which would be flower arranging and napkin folding, coupled with a brief interchange of technologies.

The first-level-of-existence meaning of "physical"

This is precisely the situation with the term "physical". We can refer to the universe as being so, but what we mean by it is open to interpretation. "No it's not" might come the reply. "It's there, I can touch it. It is three dimensional and it hurts when I bump into it." My reply is that I agree absolutely with that statement, all I intend is that we understand what we mean by it.

This "bumping into it" physical view of the universe (second level existence) is information being fed to us from our senses which are inputs to our minds. Each individual mind is a discrete element of intelligence which forms part of a collective intelligence. This I call the **Greater Intelligence** which is the source of the inputs to our minds that we call senses. It also receives outputs from our minds. It 'computes' the effect between the two and between each discrete element of intelligence such that we experience what we *call* conversation, moving about, touching table tops with our fingers, bumping into things, anything and everything that we call normal day to day living in a physical universe. Not that I'm suggesting that because we *call* these things as we do, that we are not really doing them. We are indeed doing them in every sense of the meaning, only that up till now we have not appreciated in what form of existence that we have been doing them. There is no need for machines to exist in order to compute the inputs and outputs, as per the brains in a tank model. Or, indeed any need for the brains, the tank or the water. All of existence is a state of intelligence that we refer to as the *physical universe.*

There is no need to loose sleep over whether the universe is there or not, it is and always will be because THE UNIVERSE IS WHAT IT IS. This last statement might not be fully understood but worry not, it will become clear as we move on, suffice to say it is not a play on words, it means only what it appears to.

Recap

What have I said so far? I have argued that the universe does not physically exist on the one hand, and that it does on the other. Let me make clear why I should bother contradicting myself in such a way.

Could it be that I was making a point that only clever philosophers could follow or that the meaning is so obscure that it must be the work of genius. Not quite. The fact is... I lied.

I lied in the first place by pretending that the word "physical," when used to describe the universe, really had a meaning. Namely, the preconceived version that we all think of at first. I then set about knocking down this preconceived idea only to resurrect it in its full glory after we had established its true meaning.

This technique of knocking things down and resurrecting them in full Technicolor, the self same Technicolor that was there in the first place but unseen, is one that I shall use several times to come. To be fair and so as not to insult your intelligence, I shall give due warning when I am going to use such a technique again after all, I am trying to communicate, not frustrate.

The fact is, I could hardly start part one of the book by suggesting that although we consider the universe as being physical, it is in fact pure intelligence which is in itself what we consider to be physical and by considering it as such it therefore is. It would sound complicated to say the least. My experience is that complication breeds with complication until all you have is lots of little complications running around, so I prefer to avoid it. By otherwise taking such a direct approach I would be trying to change the appearance of a preconceived idea (physical existence) by tackling it head on. Trying to 'belt' it into a different shape by assaulting the grasp the reader would already have on a well established concept only to finally reveal the same shape but more clearly defined.

No. It was much simpler to be deliberately misleading by suggesting the preconceived idea should be completely thrown out and a new one put in its place (pure intelligence). Having got that on-a-roll I then brought back the preconceived idea and demonstrated that it exactly matched the new one and therefore IS the new one, as indeed the new one is it. They are one and the same.

Like this, the "physical" school of thought get to keep their view of reality and I get to keep mine with both converging at a lower level of meaning. By which I mean: they know beyond doubt (from the *second* level existence point of view) that they are touching the table with their finger in order to convince themselves of its physical reality but they also know they cannot prove it. This is because they cannot touch the table with their mind (just as Rip'em Wesley could not get out of his submarine to touch the treasure chest for himself.) Where as, on the other hand, I also know (from the *first* level of existence point of view) that they are indeed touching a table but only because they **KNOW** it. (It is in their minds that they are touching it and therefore they **are** touching it with their minds!) I too am unable to prove it and at this point we hit common ground upon which we converge. Converging at a lower level of meaning in that we both would have to agree the other's view to be permissible because neither can be proved nor disproved, except that mine has one teeny advantage: it goes on to answer metaphysical questions like the purpose of the universe, the meaning of life, the existence of a Creator and the purpose and creation of matter, and much, much more.

These things that the "pure-intelligence form of existence" camp (first level existence) has weighted in its favour are the WHY of the universe, the HOW of which parts two to four will explain. An explanation that can be taken with or without the metaphysical reason WHY as described in this first part of the book. After all, at the end of the day, the tasty cake of 'how' tastes just the same with or without the baker relaying why he bothered to make it in the first place, but it's nice to know.

25

CHAPTER 3

THE NON-PHYSICAL UNIVERSE

Worry not if the above still sounds complicated. Let me now offer another broad swipe of the brass-rubber's crayon, with another quite separate angle that demonstrates how I can argue that the universe is the manifestation of pure intelligence on one hand, and how I can still call it physical on the other, and it starts with beer.

Overview

I am about to argue that human beings cannot know what is meant by "physical" existence until they have experienced, or been enlightened about, an alternative version of that state. Given that we only know existence in one form; that in which we experience it, we cannot possibly know what it means apart from to give it a name. The meaning is therefore open to interpretation and the interpretation I place on it is that what we experience as existence is pure intelligence that we call "physical" existence.

You only know one because you have tried the other

Many have tried a good pint of beer. But how do they know it is a good one? Answer: because they have also tried a bad one. Likewise we know "up" because we know "down." In fact, we cannot describe anything with a degree of latitude (its up/down, rough/smooth, there/not there, or anything in-between) until we have explored towards the two extremes. Indeed, we cannot realise the existence of any one thing unless we can see more than one of its faces. We know music is music because we know when it is not.

Part 1: Existence

We know water when we are paddling in it because we know when we are not. We know happiness because we have experienced moments with a less euphoric emotion. It is simply a case of sensation. Rather abstract but pure common sense.

The 'Hum' model

If we were born into a world in which all of us experienced the same continuous hum, we would not notice it. We would never have known anything different and therefore it would be of no significance. More importantly, we would be totally unaware of its existence. But why? It would be very much in existence and yet, beyond our perception. The reason is of course just as we have already said; we would not have known anything different. It would be an experience with no latitude (hum/no hum, loud hum/quiet hum) and therefore undetectable as an experience. This, of course, represents a model and one that can be clearly seen as a model because it has constraints that prevent it from being reality.

The main constraint is that the hum would not really go undetected. Modern science would reveal its existence with a microphone, amplifier and oscilloscope. Ironically, such a constraint underlines what a good model this is with respect to demonstrating the aspects for which it is intended, as we shall see in a while.

Modern science would publish pictures of the hum's wave-form produced on the oscilloscope and describe the phenomena something like this: "guess what folks, all the time we've been about there's been this thing that we are going to call a "hum" and we haven't noticed it before. This is a picture of what it looks like and so that you can see what bits of the wave-form represent the "hum," here is another picture of what we think it would look like if we could switch it off. This explains why our voices and machinery fall silent at a certain frequency. It is because the wave-form, that we and our machinery produce at that frequency, is exactly that of the "hum". And because we have 'heard' this hum since birth it is a hum which, to us, is silent and so goes our voices and machinery at that frequency. If the hum were switched off we would suddenly notice what it is we've been listening to by virtue of its absence. In other words we are deaf to the hum frequency."

It is of course true that the occupants of the 'hum world,' would eventually receive ear damage and be quite literally deaf to the hum frequency, and therefore unable to notice it when it stopped. This is a another constraint and one that should be ignored. The sort of deafness I refer to is the psychological version. Like sitting in a lovely hot bath. Keep very still and eventually it feels neither hot nor cold. You are what could be called "skin deaf" or better known as "desensitised". Your sense of feel has been robed of its latitude of experience that enables it to identify what it is experiencing. As we have already said: we cannot realise the existence of any one thing unless we can see more than one of its faces. It is simply a case of sensation, and sitting very still in the bath removes sensation.

The reason the constraint (of the hum being discovered by science) underlines so well the purpose of the model is that the scientists would have imparted the relevant latitude of experience to us by describing what the hum is like and what it is not like. They would be making us aware of the fact that it is there by showing us that it could also not be there. A latitude of experience imparted in the form of "there/not there" by describing what we would hear if it disappeared.

This is in just the same way as we only know we are *up* because we know we are not *down*. If we did not know when we were *up* because we did not know what *down* was like, and we were actually in a state of being *up*, we would still have to conclude that we were certainly *somewhere*.

After all, we would not cease to exist simply because we did not know what height we were. We would live in ignorance of our height until, that is, it changed by moving in a downward direction. We would then declare ourselves to be *down* and realise an understanding of height. Until this movement took place, being *up* would mean nothing to us even though that is precisely what our height was. In fact, the word "height" would mean nothing to us, it would be just a name.

Returning to the "hum model," that is not to say that we would undergo the actual experience of both hearing the hum and not hearing it by virtue of the enlightenment of the scientists. No. We would be enlightened not by experience but by knowledge. We would **know** of the conceivable non-existence of the hum and therefore **appreciate** its existence. A picture of the latitude-of-experience would be presented to us by the scientists albeit a latitude the "up and down" of which (hum there/hum not there) we could not actually experience for ourselves.

Conclusion

And so it is with the so called "physical" universe. We have no experience of it being anything other than just that, so to use the word physical to describe it, is meaningless in the first place. How could it be otherwise? We have no latitude of experience to give it any meaning. It is just a name. If we could experience a universe which is not physical then we would suddenly realise what we mean by one that *is* physical, just as the hum becomes apparent only when it stops.

That's not to say that the pure intelligence universe is the non-physical version that we need to be the opposite extreme to the physical and thereby impart a meaning to the word physical. No. The physical universe *is* the pure intelligence universe. Both are the same thing with no latitude of experience inferred. This is because there can only be one form of existence because all of existence is all there is and so can only be one thing. THE UNIVERSE IS WHAT IT IS.

Recap

This theory describes a universe that is pure intelligence and therefore I have to start out by describing it as not physical, but after analysis we can see that I would have as much difficulty in describing how it is not physical as the physical school of thought would have in saying it *is*, because the word is meaningless. This is because "physical" has no latitude of experience that gives it a meaning (if we knew physical and not physical we could compare the two and decide where our experience lies and thus know what we mean by physical) All that can be said is that **the universe is what it is** and if we all agree to call it physical well then that is precisely what it is.

However, I have then gone one step further to say that this universe, that we call physical, is pure intelligence of which we form part. Intelligence is something for which we do have a latitude of experience. We know clever, we know stupid. We know problem and answer. We know agree and disagree. Intelligence is mind and mind is also something for which we have a latitude of experience. Having applied the test of latitude-of-experience, it can be said that intelligence and mind are not meaningless words and what is more, they are words that describe existence. So if human beings are going to insist on using the meaningless word of "physical" in referring to existence, we must conclude that existence in the form of pure intelligence can also be called physical which then lends a meaning to it, but only by association with intelligence.

Another swipe with the crayon: I am not saying the universe is not physical and I am not saying it is. Only that it can equally be argued to be either. So if it can be regarded as both physical and not physical at the same time then the two must cancel each other out to give a word that is meaningless. But, the universe is certainly something; hence I say "THE UNIVERSE IS WHAT IT IS" and it is pure intelligence and intelligence has a latitude of experience and therefore a word that is not meaningless. Because the universe is what it is and what it is, is what we call physical, then physical has a meaning but only in association with the word intelligence.

By itself the word physical means nothing! If the universe is pure intelligence then by taking "physical" from it still leaves the universe intact. Take away "intelligence" and you are left with no universe. This suggests that physical is inert but intelligence is fundamental. You might argue that this last statement relies heavily on whether you believe the universe is pure intelligence or not. If you don't, then you could say that it is physical but then you come back to the point at which I started this controversy, namely; if the universe is physical then how do you know that for a fact. It requires the input to the mind by way of the five senses before it can decide that it is physical. The mind is undoubtedly intelligence but the mind cannot reach out and 'touch' for itself that which third party agents (the senses) are busily reporting as being physical, so how can it know?

The overwhelming evidence in favour of the pure intelligence argument is that it answers the unanswerable questions that man has hither to set himself, both in terms of a higher being, the meaning of life, life after death, etc., on one hand, and scientific observation on the other (all of which will be revealed in this book and the others in the series). The overwhelming argument against the physical (not pure intelligence universe) is that rather then answering the questions, it sets them - judge for yourself.

The Ultimate Explanation

Having got over this rather complicated philosophical issue, I promise the remainder is a lot less bumpy. The fact that the universe is what it is and the answer to the question of what exactly it *is*, is one that will make itself evident in a more subtle fashion as we move through the rest of the book.

CHAPTER 4
THE MEANING OF LIFE

The view I have given of first level existence is one in which all of creation is the manifestation of pure intelligence which I collectively term The Greater Intelligence, of which we each form part. Therefore, our role in such a system is to process data as data processing sub-units within that intelligence. In other words; our job is to process data - which is *the act of being intelligent*. Given that all of creation is intelligence and we form part of that intelligence within it, we are effectively mini images of all creation, created in its image. This can be best explained from the second level existence perspective as follows. (Second level existence being how the universe appears to us. As being solid and separate from our minds. Not pure intelligence. Although first level existence shows that the two are the same, see figure one on page 12).

So, from the second level existence point of view, the raw data that we receive is everything that enters our minds by way of our senses. The data we output is the result of our decisions by way of our movement, manipulation and communication etc. Both input and output is the result of interfacing with the physical universe (remembering that we are talking "second level existence"). The data processing that goes on in between receiving data and delivering outputs is what we do in our minds. Decision making in other words.

Every item within the universe with which we interface is the product of intelligence that we process by interfacing with it. By picking up any object and placing it elsewhere, we are processing data. We are manipulating intelligence such that the Greater Intelligence is thinking because ultimately everything IS the Greater Intelligence. Everything we do is the manipulation of data and everything we decide to do is the processing of data by the act of making a decision. It can be said that the Greater Intelligence is all knowing, all powerful and omnipresent. It can be said to take on these attributes in the form of a collective intelligence, not simply as a single intellectual entity.

The Greater Intelligence is not composed only of us as its data processing sub units but every object in the universe and thereby consisting of the universe as an entirety. Which is all of creation. The question now has to be asked; if the entire universe is really one giant brain, as it were, what is it thinking about and for what purpose? In this respect there are two things we can be sure of. Firstly, that it does not think as we do, and secondly, it does not think as one entity.

It cannot think as we do because the difference in ability between it and any one of us is as big as the universe is broad, just as a dust bug does not think as we do due to the difference in sophistication. It cannot be a single entity because if it were, it would ultimately be all there is, in terms of a 'thinking thing,' and therefore not able to communicate with anything else. As such there would be no input or outputs and nothing to process; to think about. It would therefore be incapable of thought because it would have no thoughts to think. It would not 'talk' to itself because it would have nothing to talk about.

How can I be so bold as to assume such logic? By the power of logic itself, which dictates the following: that if we are made in its image, then as its image we can look to ourselves for guidance as to its form. Inversely, if we collectively form the Greater Intelligence, then it can but take OUR image. Just as England is made up of the English. Fill it full of the French and you have France that used to be called England. And like a nation, it is so much more powerful than the individual even though it is formed by precisely that.

However the Greater Intelligence might perform its thinking process, we can be certain it does it as a mass of intellectual entities. Like an embryo formed by numerous cells, it would consist of intelligences talking to more of the same within the same overall intelligence. We may well be those very same intellectual entities, all 'talking' to each other and all collectively forming part of the Greater Intelligence. Then on the other hand, there may well be something in between. One way or another this is another topic and one that I shall return to in book four but for now I can tell you that logic dictates that there is indeed something in between.

We are therefore data processing sub units of a greater data-processing system that I call the Greater Intelligence. This is our purpose which also tells us what we are. The other grand question of "where are we?" can now be answered. Quite simply, we are nowhere. We are within a system of intelligence supported by a structure of no three-dimensional constraints; a system of pure intelligence. How this is the case will be identified and demonstrated in parts four and five. I must stress that we are not glorified calculators, however. We are indeed every bit as clever as we think we are. "The Mind of Our Creator" in part five, will return to this point but essentially; processing data, at the human level, is very much more than being a computer on legs. Processing data is, in itself, the act of being intelligent. Part five will address the question of what The Greater intelligence is thinking about. It will also touch upon how our intelligence is central to the workings of the universe. But before I can make those statements we first have some considerable ground to cover in order that they should make sense.

Logic

The universe (second level existence universe, that is) is often described as a cosmos which means exactly the opposite to chaos. For "cosmos" read "logic." It is a system which follows rules and is therefore predictable. This is because it is a rational, logical, thinking system that if it where not so would produce chaos and disorder (entropy will be addressed in book 2). Such logic makes itself evident in rules like "opposite poles attract and like poles repel" when talking of magnetism. They always do, we know we can depend on it, so much so that we can design motors based on such a principle. The examples are endless and precisely what you would expect of a system that 'crunches' data in a logical fashion.

Free will

I would hate to upset people by painting a picture of a human being as nothing more then a glorified calculator. This is not what I intend. We are as clever as we think we are. We can reason, communicate and generally flex our logical muscles along with the best of them. But the very process of doing just that is unavoidably the act of processing data.

We do nothing without it being based on a decision, or someone else's decision. For example, "I decided to jump" or "he decided to push me". Every such decision is based on what we know at the time, which is derived from all our previous experiences. These experiences are inputs to the mind, whatever they might be, however they might manifest themselves, typically; opinions, beliefs, emotions, fears, memories, reflexes, etc., etc. Given what we know at any one instant, we will then make a decision to do a certain something that would be the same certain something no matter how many times the history of the universe was re-run up to the point of making that decision. I would decide to jump every time, or equally, I would always be in exactly that spot when he would always decide to push me.

In conclusion, although we have free will to decide what to do, we will only do what our previous experiences dictate we should by processing those experiences to produce a decision. That being the case, the final decision we make is one that must have been intrinsic in the previous experiences, a certain set of which will dictate a foregone result. If a different result was obtained then it could only be as a result of a different set of experiences.

The mind of the Greater Intelligence

We are now getting a feel for how the mind of this Greater Intelligence is working (not forgetting that it is a mind collectively formed by many individual minds). For instance, we know that it has to think one thought after another; in a serial fashion. Albeit that it would think many of these serial thoughts in parallel, the fact remains that each smallest element of data has to be processed one at a time. Five swimmers racing across the pool, all swimming in parallel but each has no choice but to make one stroke after the other in a serial fashion.

If the Greater Intelligence could think all its thoughts in parallel, it would do so in one instant and thereby have thought all the thoughts it was ever going to think in one instantaneous flurry of parallel activity. This would render its data processing sub units (us) as redundant and therefore non-existent, which we know for sure we are not. As René Descartes put it, "I think therefore I am." And the "am" in which we "are" is as discrete data processors all processing our data (by living what we see as our normal every day lives) in a serial type fashion.

CHAPTER 5
RECAP AND CONCLUSION TO
PART ONE

Given that this is an **holistic** theory (in that it is explaining and taking the view of the entire picture and not discrete elements of it) it will be seen as being in total reflection of this fact when I say that the argument should not be taken as conclusive or convincing thus far. It is as the total picture of all creation is unrolled (as straight forwardly as I can) that all its parts will demonstrate themselves as supporting all the others. This then, and when in total possession of the overall picture, is when the reader will be able to judge the proof of what will otherwise seem, at times, to be too fantastic for credence. For now I am simply "telling it like it is" and allow the rest of this ultimate explanation to demonstrate it to be the simple truth.

To do this, first level existence will now take a back seat. I do not expect to have convinced or explained fully this mind boggling concept in just this part of the book. That will now happen of its own accord as I embark on an explanation of the second level existence universe.

After the first part of the book, I shall embark on an explanation of the overall scheme of things from the view point that we all understand, i.e. the universe as being purely as it appears, as being separate from our minds and being a thing that does not have intelligence in its own right. I am going to place the universe right back into the lap of the "Physical-universe school of thought" and pretend that the word physical has a meaning of the preconceived form. This I will do simply by referring to it as the second level existence universe because that is precisely what that term means. (See figure one on page 12).

But the fact that the universe is a logical cosmos in which we have "free will" to decide (compute) by way of our knowledge (previous experience) what patterns it follows, is something that can be directly translated across from its true reality to its apparent second level reality. These patterns are described by theories and models many of which exist and all of which will never be anything more than just that; theories and models. To paraphrase Einstein: "we can look at the watch and theorise on its workings but we can never look inside to know how it truly works." Given an understanding of first and second level existence, we can now see how true this statement is. Simply because the second level existence watch does not exist. Second level existence, which part two will begin to explain, is just as much a model as existing theories but it is a model that covers all of creation and not parts of it in isolation. It is a model the constraints of which I shall identify and from which I shall again describe true reality (first level existence) the tip of which we have only scraped in part one. The entire iceberg will become self evident as we move through an explanation of the second level existence universe.

To do this I will hold first level existence in the background and repeatedly pull it out to wave like a winning ticket at the races, to demonstrate how this provides the hitherto unseen reason 'why' behind the various aspects of the universe. Sixty five million dollars on-the-nose; of an invisible horse that will be seen to win the race when the vision is correctly focused, the same focusing which will reveal the emperors, riding the other horses, as wearing no clothes. Needless to add that the rider of our horse is none other than Rip'em Wesley: jockey extraordinair !

****

CHAPTER 6
PHILOSOPHY OF THEORIES

As we reach the end of part one, I shall now take this opportunity to make clear my stance with respect to the idea of a theory that explains the 'how' of the second level existence universe in the form of a prelude to the rest of the book.

As I have said before, the universe that we perceive is a model (the *ultimate* model of reality) that implies true reality with true reality being first level existence which is pure intelligence (see figure one on page 12). Therefore, whatever I have to say on the subject of the second level existence universe must be by way of a model and not reality itself, as is the case for all existing and future theories. This is very much not the case for first level existence which *is* true reality and not a model of it. An understanding of first level existence gives us the absolute reason 'why' behind all of creation, the 'how' of which is described by second level existence (again, I recommend a look at figure one).

As a model, the second level existence part of this theory is as viable as any of the existing models (the Big Bang Theory, to name but one) that each goes to explain the separate parts of the same ultimate model. As such, it in no way displaces them, it simply works in parallel with them. After all, when it comes to explaining *anything* it is always the case that there is more than one way of explaining it. By which I mean that there is always more than one way of looking at (or modelling) the same reality.

Make no mistake, this is not an excuse for being so bold as to attempt to answer the ultimate questions, it is a statement of fact. Existing theories, which are reductionistic (tackling parts of, and not the whole of) are often seen as each insisting that they are the correct interpretation of reality. What they fail to realise is that the reality they are each referring to, is only a model in the first place. What *I* am saying, on the other hand, is that *all* theories are viable for the very reason that reality, as we see it, is precisely that - *a model*, albeit the ultimate model.

This theory is holistic in that it tackles the entire picture, presenting a single unified vision that lends itself to *all* phenomena. Be that the case then it must **in**clude, and not **ex**clude, existing ideas and theories as being analogous (..model of) the same true reality that we each seek to explain.

Time is a good example of this: in the next part of the book I shall argue that time is not a dimension, it is simply the phenomena of movement which is already spoken for by way of other dimensions; up/down, backward/forward, left/right. I shall be seen to be quite insistent on this point but this is all within the view point of reality that *this* theory seeks to explain. If other models successfully match observation by use of time as a dimension, then I cannot possibly say they are wrong. Just that they are each a different way of looking at the same thing.

This means that if someone said that Einstein, by including the use of time as a dimension, successfully explained the deflection of light by a star, then I would totally agree. On the other hand, if that same person insisted that my explanation for the same effect (explained in book two) is wrong because it does *not* require time to be dimensional, I would then have to disagree. But the reason for disagreeing is not simply a case of who is wrong and who is right about time being a dimension. It is more subtle than that.

Let me explain: if I stepped into the Einstein camp then I would say it is correct that time should be dimensional. If I stepped back to my own camp I would say it is not dimensional. Each statement would be correct because each camp is modelling the same reality. But to look from one camp to the other and make comparisons about who is right or wrong, is a nonsensical exercise. We each serve to explain the same reality but do it in different ways. The only way to draw a comparison between the two is to say that each is analogous of the other. They must be if they achieve the same result (with the result being to match observation).

Further - on the point of who is right or wrong - even if two theories each predicted *different* observations, then, if their logic is reasonable, they must *still* both be correct but by varying degrees. Einstein himself made this point about Newton's theory of gravity. To paraphrase him: it is not the case that Newton is wrong but that his own version is more correct. Like this, Newton's theory fits within Einstein's as being analogous of it: it models it; it implies it. This fell on deaf ears for the most part with the declaration that the mechanical view (Newton's and before) is dead and the field (..etc.) view is alive. They are *both* alive accept that the latter is more holistic than the other.

Newton also said this of his predecessors by way of his famous quote that he was able to see further than others by standing on the shoulders of giants. Newton and Einstein were not being modest by paying tribute to their predecessors. They meant what they said! If the giants upon whose shoulders Newton stood were dead, then Newton would have seen no further than the giant's floored shoulders would allow. And so too with Einstein.

If someone said that the earth is sticky and that is why we remain upon it, in a sense he would be correct but Einstein and Newton would be more correct in their analysis of the same result. The "sticking" idea would be viable just as theirs is and so it must form part of their thinking. It is not displaced by it.

Or, by the same token, if that someone also said that light was a sort of bright thinga-me-jig that shines out such that it makes objects that get in its way "sort of bright" as well then he would not be wrong. He would be just as right as the more academically acceptable description of the same effect. It is not the case that anything is dead in order that something else can live in its place. It is just that one is more correctly applicable and therefore better to work with when trying to advance knowledge on that subject.

Now I am not for one minute suggesting that the rest of this book is going to present an explanation that is as crass as the examples just given. Only that it does not wipe out any other existing theories.

Long live the big bang, Einstein, Newton and all!

And if theirs are considered more correct than mine - long live mine.

PART 2

SPACE & TIME

The existing three dimensions are up/down, left/right, back-ward/forward. They infer the existence of a fourth. Time is non-dimensional and therefore not the fourth. The universe must be four dimensional in order to facilitate a universe that folds in on itself. We know the universe must fold in on itself because there is no such thing as nothing with which to otherwise form a boundary to something which is only three dimensional.

CHAPTER 1

BUILDING BLOCKS

Having roughly established the first level existence background and its logical nature in part one, part two will now begin the task of addressing the apparent second level existence universe by establishing just three simple rules. These rules form the primary building blocks for the construction of a new universal theory.

<u>Three Simple Rules</u>

1. First there is existence (second level).
2. Then there is movement.
3. Then there is everything in the universe as derived from the first two.

These rules are telling us that anything that figures as a part of creation must exist in the first place. Then, to have any effect within creation they must move. And finally, anything and everything, from object to phenomena, is as a result of existing and moving.

Sounds like gross over simplification. Absolutely. Why should the universe be anything other than simple ? Needless to say, there are certain subtleties that require to be understood. Existence is not quite as it appears, as we have uncovered in part one. Then there is the subject of movement. This too is not quite as it appears. It is in fact four dimensional and not three dimensional. Within this four dimensional movement lies the heart of every phenomena in the entire universe but to see how this rather mind blowing generalisation is the case, we need first to understand what these four dimensions are. In particular we need to identify the fourth (which is not time) and the best way to establish that is to understand the first three conventionally accepted dimensions and see how they dictate the existence of a fourth.

After all, if this theory is as I claim it to be; simple and holistic, then you would expect this new fourth dimension to be nothing more than obvious and inextricably linked to the first three. This is precisely what it is. It forms a straight forward extension to them and bares all their existing characteristics. It is energy. Energy is the fourth dimension, in fact energy is the first, second, third and fourth dimension as will be explained. The concept of energy will be so thoroughly courted between the confines of our imagination and these pages, that "wedding bells are go'na chime!"

But first - 'Chocolates for the future mother-in-law' in the form of this; part two, in which we will explore the case for such a concept. How logic tells us that there is a fourth dimension and how it is very much not time (within this theory). Energy as the fourth dimension will be specifically discussed in part three, to reveal the shape, nature and structure of the universe, and show how energy forms the pure intelligence fabric of the first-level-existence Greater Intelligence. Gradually the above three very simple rules, for all of creation, will be bolstered by the fortification of some very simplistic logic. For now we need a clear reason for the existence of this fourth dimension.

CHAPTER 2
THREE DIMENSIONS

Overview

A discussion of the three conventional dimensions now follows, explaining what they are and reasoning that none of these dimensions can exist if any of them are removed. This will demonstrate, by a logical, philosophical process, how they are in fact one, the subdivision into three being purely academic; for the sake of explanation, lending itself to text books, not the real world (real as in second level existence of course).

What are they?

Up/down, left/right, backward/forward. A line is one dimensional, a disc is two dimensional and a sphere is three dimensional. A straight line on a piece of paper is one dimensional, the sheet of paper itself is two and a box is three. Any solid object is made up of three dimensions: height, width and depth.

Co-ordinates are also three dimensional: "go along the road towards the beach, go up two levels in the car park and head past all the pay and display machines running parallel with the beach.... and if you don't get parked you shouldn't shop on Christmas eve."

Not three, but one

All very simple; "there are three dimensions," just as published by the institute of conventional belief. We are taught it at school and perpetuate it at work and adult life but I would have to argue that it isn't that simple. It is very complicated and confusing in fact because in the real world it quite simply is not true. There is only one dimension!

Let's have a look at a cube and ask what would be left if we took away one of these three dimensions from which it is formed, say, height. Logic would suggest it might reduce to a flat square area. If this is logic then best we don't use it for anything other than Tax Returns - if the height is removed nothing is left!

A flat square area with no height is not possible. "Flat" is a fictitious single dimensional description for use in coaching a child through the process of appreciating what goes into the formation of an object, typically represented by a box. A box which has been reduced to one of its six sides (a sheet of cardboard) to highlight two of the so called three dimensions that forms it and any other structure that the child might care to think of. A process of teaching that is without fault but what the child does not always go on to appreciate as an adult is that the sheet of cardboard has height without which it would not exist. By removing its height, it can be seen that its width and depth also disappears. In fact the removal of *any* one dimension removes the other two.

Now, I know this sounds like a case of taking things too literally. It could very well be said: "everyone knows that the sheet of cardboard would, of course, have to have height. It is just a way of explaining one of the three dimensions." But it is a pity that the fact that this is only an explanation is not as well appreciated as the three dimensions themselves. That explanation does not transpose into the real world.

My point is this. If all of the three dimensions disappear with the removal of just one, then they must all be one dimension in the first place. That being the case, how can a one dimensional object be that of three dimensions? There is nothing in this universe that exists in less than these so called three dimensions. They only exist separately of one another in the fictitious form within the binding of text books - noble literature designed to describe the real world by using fictitious dimensions that do not exist in the real world. Hmm? There in lies a contradiction and one that gave my simple little brain (that still is) great problems as a child.

While little mister "look at my stunning mathematical abilities" was winning a bladed dual between sharpened pencil and crowded exam paper, I screwed mine up with whitened knuckles. I never could take to that bloody Wesley kid.

Any way, the same goes for co-ordinations. If you were asked to point to the location of the spare car park slot mentioned above, you would stick your finger in precisely its direction. You would not perform peculiar gesticulations with your finger first pointing forward towards the beach then up in the air and finally along to the left. Certainly the final indication of location is composed of these three movements, but only in theory. They do not work in the real world. Try it. The finger finishes pointing to the left and that is not where the parking slot is relative to where you are standing.

I am not saying we are wrong to use three separate fictitious entities to describe real world objects or locations. But to then say that those real world objects or locations are composed of three separate entities which are not fictitious but real, is very wrong. All three dimensions together are real, any one or two dimensions in isolation of all three are make-believe. Any object or location in real-world-terms is therefore the manifestation of a single dimension which can then be theoretically described by the use of three *fictitious* dimensions.

Recap

My poor simple brain has suffered over the years, which has driven me to explain things in my own unambiguous terms in order that I can accept them. I am highly sensitive to ambiguity which often results in making me appear slow with an uncanny ability to complicate things. Ironically, this is exactly the trend that I seek to reverse. The apparent complication comes from being unconventional which is very much the case here.

It is very simple, "If it don't make for good logic, then it don't make for anything." In this instance we have, on one hand, a single object being explained by three separate dimensions (fine, no problem with that: *as an explanation*, but;) on the other hand the same object is then said to manifest itself in the real world by virtue of exactly those three separate dimensions (now enter the ambiguity:) even, that is, in light of the fact that if you remove one, the others all disappear. To pin point the ambiguity: are all three really one or are they three?

My answer is this. It makes sense to me that if the three cannot be separated, then there must be a seamless joint between them, and something without joints is one, not several. This "one" (whole item), as I see it, can certainly be explained; taught; described; measured by the use of several make-believe parts but to then treat each of those make-believe parts as being independently real, is just not logically possible. They must therefore be one and the "one" that they are is volume, a volume that is measured by three independently fictitious dimensions that collectively provide for a real volumetric whole.

Simplicity

As I come across various theories that attempt to explain parts of reality by the introduction of more and more dimensions, I cannot help but conclude that as an intelligence, the human race is looking in the 'labour-intensive' direction for explanation. In the direction of complication, while the simplistic route lies in serene opposition, arrogant with silent explanation.

I prefer the simplistic route of reducing three dimensions to one. In fact, to take this route of simplicity one step further, and to be fair, I must tell you that in part three I will extend the above logic to show the three dimensions of volume to be three quarters of the ultimate single dimension of density, of which energy is the fourth quarter. That will be it, this is not a progressive affair. Give no thought to energy or density at this stage. I mention them now for three reasons the first of which is in a sustained effort to show where I am taking you (as opposed to stringing-out the mystery). Secondly, so as not to loose your confidence and thirdly, because I couldn't resist. Without doing so would mean each time I present something as appearing to be the final picture you will always wonder if I am going to change it again. This is rather like the technique of knocking things down only to resurrect them in their full glory, as described in part one. Having done it once, I do not intend to repeat it without giving due warning.

CHAPTER 3
SPACE AND THE NEED FOR A
FOURTH DIMENSION

Overview

The intention within this chapter is to disprove the concept of space as being empty by offering the logic that there is no such thing as nothing. This being the case, it is impossible for a three dimensional universe to have an edge because there is no such thing as nothing with which to form an edge. This therefore endorses the need for a fourth dimension that provides a universe with no edge, provided by virtue of folding in on itself.

Empty space

This really has to be one of the greatest ambiguities I have come across. On the one hand the space that lies beyond the atmosphere of our planet is said to be empty, and on the other; there is something there that goes by the name of "space". It is one of the profoundest insults to common sense to suggest that space is empty. I make no bones about it: this is a classic case of the "Emperor's clothes are missing." I start with this opening logic: if there were truly nothing between two objects, they would have to be touching, not separated by something!

Empty space is said to exist between astronomical bodies at the macroscopic level and between atomic particles at the microscopic level. From a purely logical point of view, it has to be argued that if nothing exists then there can't be any such thing as nothing for it to exist in the first place.

Let me run that by you again, although you have probably read it several times by now. What I mean is that to describe something as not being there, means that it is not there to describe. So, to say that nothing lies between two bodies (whatever those bodies might be) is to give that "nothing" a location; position; dimension; an existence and that is not possible if it does not exist. Nothing does not exist by virtue of its own definition.

Once again, I do not intend that the above brief argument should be sufficient or in anyway conclusive. I am battling against an established convention, the very same battle that others have tried to fight before in the form of space either not being empty (but not knowing with what it is then full of) or being very nearly empty. I too am suggesting that it is full. Full to the brim with not the smallest gap of so called nothing. It is full with none other than energy (an **ether of energy**) and in such a way as to provide gravitation, the fourth dimension and the formation of matter. That is where my ammunition will come from as parts three and four will explain. Part five will address the Michelson-Morley experiment which is supposed to disprove the existence of an ether. For now I will persist with this almost child like simplistic argument that sets the scene with unambiguous logic, the back bone of which is what will become a golden rule: THERE IS NO SUCH THING AS NOTHING!

The edge of the universe

To further illustrate the point that there is no such thing as nothing I now invite you on a private journey to the edge of the universe. We will see what is to be found there.

We depart from our planet Earth with no space ship, no space suit, just ourselves (yes; another one of those thought experiments). We head out from our solar system, on out of the Milky Way galaxy and towards the other galaxies that lay beyond. Past those and onward, ever onward until finally we meet with the edge of the universe. But what forms this boundary that encloses the entire universe? Nothing? Well, ok. let's let it go at that and see what logic dictates. We might decide to step through it but how can we? There is nothing there into which to step. In that case something must stop us but there is nothing to stop us. Ok, let's assume that there is a wall there. Problem: what forms the outside edge of the wall? It can't be nothing because for the wall to exist as something it must have both an inside edge and an outside edge, and the outside edge is now supposed to be the nothing, the boundary of which the wall is forming.

Right, let's suppose there is no wall, just nothing; black empty nothing that starts at the boundary. Fine, in that case I suggest a step into nothing given that there is now nothing to stop us. We stride across the boundary and place one foot into glorious nothingness. But how can this be? If there is nothing there, how can we step into it. There must be something there to accommodate our step. For that matter, if we can move into this so called nothingness, there is nothing to stop planets, galaxies or meteorites from moving into it and thereby constituting an extension to the universe. But this is more of the universe which is very much 'something,' not more of nothing and nothing is most definitely nothing.

I could carry on but I'm sure you would rather I didn't. The point is this. All that exists (which is all of creation) cannot be bound. It cannot have a boundary for the simple reason that nothing cannot exist. But the question still remains, what lies at the outermost extension to the universe. Unless, that is, it has no boundary. An infinite universe that stretches on forever.

The never ending universe

There is only one way to consider the feasibility of an infinite universe and that is to first ask the question; is there such a thing as an infinite anything?

There are two types of infinity; a linear infinity which stretches on forever, and a closed infinity like the circumference of a circle, which if it where journeyed, would go on forever - just as it is possible to journey round the earth forever. A universe that stretches on in all directions forever, is a linear infinity. But is it really possible? Although I am about to discuss this at length, I will state up-front that I don't believe it is. I cannot see that there is an infinite anything other then a closed infinity.

Linear infinity

Something that stretches on forever in the form of a linear infinity, cannot have an end. That is to say, it cannot be continuously in the act of getting longer because this would require that that it should have an end with which to be getting longer with, and if it stretches on forever it cannot have an end. So anything which is said to have a linear infinity must be as big as it is ever going to get. Likewise, it must be in a state where by it is not going to get smaller because that would also need an end with which to get smaller with.

The universe is said to be expanding. I agree with this. In fact we will see later how it cannot *help* but expand. But for now it has to be said that if it is expanding then it is getting bigger and so it must have a front with which to be getting bigger with, which shows that it is not as big as it is ever going to get. That rather kills the idea of an infinitely extending universe as logically dead as dead can be.

To be fair, it could be said that if this logic is truly rugged then what if the universe is, as some people also believe it to be, not expanding but in a steady state. The logic should be equally applicable whether I happen to agree with a universe which is expanding or not. (Although, I will demonstrate in part five how the universe can be expanding and yet still be in a "steady state")

In the case of the non-expanding (steady state) universe, we would have to be considering the matter that populates the universe as being that which is extending on forever, not the space in which it sits because that is supposed to be nothing. If this nothing *was* supposed to stretch on forever, that would then suggest that the matter would eventually have to run out, leaving empty space to stretch onwards infinitum. That would have to be nonsense because space with nothing in it is nothing and there is no such thing as nothing. So if matter eventually runs out, then the universe it forms cannot run on forever. Empty space cannot run on forever because that is nothing and there is no such thing as nothing. So to be talking of a universe that stretches on forever, we must be considering the matter in it as populating the universe forever onwards - an infinite amount of matter.

This infinite amount of matter would need to be as explained above - an amount of matter which is as much as it is ever going to be, with no prospect of getting less or more. This must be the case if it is infinite. If it were not as much as it was ever going to be, then it must be a finite amount of matter to which is going to be added more matter on its way to infinity. If it has not reached infinity then it must be finite.

A universe consisting of an infinite amount of matter means that no more matter can be added because there is as much as there can ever be. So if you can spot an area of space that can accommodate additional matter, then you have just proved the universe is not an infinite extension of matter because it has not finished accruing all the matter that it can before it can declare itself saturated with matter and therefore infinite. All this so called empty space that is

57

supposed to occupy the universe seems to provide plenty of scope in which to slide even the tiniest additional matter. So if it has not reached infinity yet, it must still be finite with an ever growing front of additional matter.

Besides, if what we are talking about is all of creation, which we are, then from where is all this matter coming from to enable the universe to reach a state of having an infinite amount of matter? It cannot be coming from itself, that defeats logic. Just as we cannot pick ourselves up by our own boot laces. Likewise, it cannot be argued that there is alternative universes (i.e., more then one "all of creation") because I would then ask what separates them. Nothing? "there ain't no such thing," therefore they must constitute the same whole. Besides *all* of creation means precisely that.

The closed infinity

All of the above discussion should not really be necessary. It offends common sense to think of anything that stretches on forever. It smacks of being a "cop-out". Something like: "well I don't know what's at the edge of the universe or what would constitute the boundary if it did have an edge so let's just say it goes on forever". Sorry. Not good enough! It has an extension in the form of three dimensions that can't have an end because there is no such thing as nothing to be beyond it and therefore the suggestion is nonsensical. It can't stretch on forever because that is equally nonsensical. So we are left with the only viable option open to us: our recently aquatinted friend "the closed infinity".

Taking the example given earlier; that of a circle's circumference, we find that this would translate across nicely to solve the conundrum of a three dimensional shape we call the universe, that has no edge and yet appears to go on forever. Obviously it would not be a circle but it would certainly be circular by nature. As you set off from the planet

Earth and head out again towards what you would expect to be the edge, you would find, this time, that it never appears. Just like the circle, you would simply keep going.

The circle has a circumference that provides a walkway of endless repetition. Whatever arbitrary point is considered to be the start of one's journey, is the start of a trail that curves round to end at its origin by way of a seamless joint. And so it must be with the shape of the universe. It must somehow fold in on itself to end at its origin to provide a journey that would go on infinitum.

The need for a fourth dimension

But this "folding in affair" cannot be accommodated by just the three conventional three dimensions that provide the extension of the universe out into three different directions in the form of volume. By using just three dimensions we would have to be talking of a sphere with its outside edge curving in to meet with the centre and that is inconceivable.

Such a characteristic can only be facilitated by a fourth dimension. A dimension which, when combined with the other three, would bend in to form both the centre and edge, in such a way as to be as obvious as the day is long. Something that is as straight forward as the volume that the first three dimensions form. A fourth dimension that does not require heaps of maths or an obscure and questionable angle on reality that can only be understood by the acquisition of numerous qualifications. This "something" will be explained in part three as being nothing more than energy. The energy that goes to make matter, that in the form of the three dimensions of volume, makes density. We shall see how such a four dimensional every day phenomena can provide a shape that curves in on itself but for now we can see a need for it to do so.

A closed system with no gaps

With a universe in which the edge and centre are one and the same, we have a closed system. And given that there is no such thing as nothing, it must be a closed system with no gaps because there is no such thing as nothing with which to form a gap. A good example of what is meant by closed in this context is to think of a pipe full of water which has a pressure gauge at one end and sealed at the other. If the pipe is heated, then the pressure indicated on the gauge goes up because it is a closed system. If the sealed end of the pipe was opened to atmosphere and held such that the water does not run out, then by heating the pipe, the pressure does not go up because the water simply expands out through the open end of the pipe (not to mention the fact that you would burn your hands). It is said to be an open system.

If the same system is sealed with air inside, as well as water, it can be said to be a closed system with a gap in it. Heating the pipe would cause the water to expand and the air bubble to contract against the pressure of the water. The gauge reading would go up very little. With no air bubbles in, it would be a closed system with no gaps.

The essence of a closed system is a system in which a disturbance at any one place within it is transmitted throughout the rest. It is important to see how the universe is a closed system with no gaps because this is what supports the effect of gravity. We will, in part three, see for the first time what transmits gravity through this so called empty space and exactly the reason why it should perform as Einstein and Newton said it should. We will also, in part three, go over how this constitutes a closed system yet again in light of what that part has to tell us.

CHAPTER 4

TIME: THE FOURTH DIMENSION?

It will be suggested here that the mysteries of time be dispelled by realising that time as a dimension doesn't exist as follows:

It can be seen that when analysed, there is no form of measurement of time that exists separately from the measurement of movement. What else is there to be said. Take away the function of movement from any time keeping device and "it don't tell the time."

Time has been invented by man and is no more than the standard rate of change of position of an object through space. Put in its simplest terms; the hands of a clock round a clock-face. All based on the movements of our planet relative to the sun and finely tuned by atomic vibrations (which is movement).

To address the popular misconception that movement is impossible without a change in time: this is like me inventing the dimension of "carrots". I could easily say that nothing can exist unless carrots exist. Nonsense you would rightly reply. If every carrot in the world was destroyed then it could be shown that we still existed and therefore prove me wrong. "No," I would say, "by destroying every carrot in the world you would actually cease to exist." Who, in their right mind is then going to destroy every carrot in the world to prove the case. No one. Therefore I could not be proven wrong. Why stop at carrots? I could invent all sorts of nonsense that no one could prove to be wrong and go on doing so all day long, being seen to be ridiculous as well. But no more ridiculous than suggesting that time is needed to enable movement.

The Ultimate Explanation

It is often said that a three dimensional object exists not only because it has three dimensions but also because it has a location in space described by those same three dimensions *at a certain point in time.* For example, at twelve o'clock the object sat at one three dimensional location and at one o'clock it was moved to another. Sure enough. But this is movement by a another name. First it is in one location, then it has moved to another, all as compared to the standard rate of change of position of a hand as it *moves* around a graduated dial. When the hand points to one position the object is in one location, when the hand reaches another position the object in question has since been moved to another location. If time stops, then all that happens is that the hand on the graduated dial stops moving. Time as in "telling the time" has stopped. The object still exists and can still be moved. Movement is movement full stop.

Compare this to removing the dimension of height. The object certainly would disappear (cease to exist). This is a viable extension to the other two dimensions of width and depth. It directly interacts with them. Time, on the other hand, is suspect to say the least as a viable extension to the existing three. They are not the remotest bit interested in interacting with this quite separate object upon which two hands rotate round a circular dial called a clock.

To then argue that movement is by virtue of time, is to beg the question of what exactly is time, other than a standard rate of movement. If someone could tell me this I might start to see how it can be construed as a dimension. At this point the cupboard of principle is thrown open wide and the tautologies are brought out. A tautology is something which is described by virtue of itself. A poor pauper for instance. He would have to be poor to be a pauper. And so it is with time. People often say "time is that which ticks by as movement takes place, and movement takes place because time ticks by." This is a null and void argument. It does not tell me what time is. Instead it goes round and round in order to justify itself by virtue of itself. Given that no description can be placed on time, other than being that which goes quickly or slowly depending on its velocity relative to the observer or indeed depending on if you are having a bad day or not (all of which is a tautology) I can only think I am wasting my time by pursuing it at all. It rattles round my head like a dry pea!

You may note that I agree it can vary according to velocity. Indeed, this is what Einstein went to great lengths to explain along with the fact that it changes in the presence of a gravitational field. None of which I could possibly deny. In fact my next book will support this, but, it will also show that it is the effect of movement (indicating the rate at which 'time' has past) that distorts, not time as a dimension in its own right.

Again I make the point as I did at the end of part one, chapter six, "Philosophy of Theories" that this is all within the context of this theory and as such I am correct in arguing that time is non-dimensional and defend it by whatever logic I choose. From the view of any other theory, that treats time as a dimension, I would agree that it too is correct - *within the confines of that theory*. All theories are describing the same reality from different angles, with each being viable.

Apparent phenomena

Within the context of this theory, the suggestion that time is nothing more then a standard rate of change of position is in much the same way that Newton (and Galileo, after a fashion) solved the problem of the unknown force that continually propelled an object through space in the absence of friction. He simply stated that it was the absence of any other force to stop it. Not that I am declaring my self to be a second 'Newton.' I am simply making the point that just because there is an apparent phenomena doesn't mean it is anything more than apparent. In this case the apparent phenomena is that of time.

Now, I know this argument appears weak to say the least and I am not the first person to try and make it. It is a personal opinion and one for which I have good reason to believe. To this end I would suggest that if the idea of time as not being a dimension is unpalatable then time can be left as being regarded as the fourth dimension and the fourth dimension of energy, introduced in part three, can be termed as a fifth dimension. It makes little difference. It will eventually be seen from this and subsequent books, that time, as a dimension, is simply not needed to describe the universe and thus becomes redundant of its own accord. This is where the real weight of my ammunition lies.

Needless to say, its "short-form, high-level language" use as a man-made standard rate-of-change-of-position reference tool is invaluable and always will be. By which I mean that we still need to know what time of day it is or how long an experiment has taken without having to relate to how far the Earth has rotated relative to the Sun since we last looked or how many inches a hand has moved whilst travelling at a standard speed round the face of a graduated dial. It is a lot easier to refer to that man made derived unit of time.

CHAPTER 5
RECAP AND CONCLUSION
TO PART TWO

Part two has started to define certain parameters based on pure logic. I have said that there are four dimensions to avoid having to have an edge to the universe or a universe that stretches on forever. I have said that the first three dimensions are really one because everything that exists does so in the form of a volumetric shape. I have also said that time does not exist as a dimension. But this is all in an effort to describe the apparent universe which, in itself, is a model. That is; the ultimate model that I have called the **second level existence universe** which in its true form is really pure intelligence. So the rules I am outlining can be taken or left, they are all open to personal interpretation. They are describing a model of reality, not reality itself, and there is always more than one way to describe anything.

If reality is really pure intelligence and that is all there is to it, then why am I bothering to describe it at all? The reason is that the universe we perceive is a description of reality and by describing it we then have a picture of how true reality works (in the form of first level existence). And that picture only makes sense if the description is an holistic one. One that encompasses everything, not fragmented elements of it as we have at present. This is where the strength of *this* description, that starts with this second part of the book, lies, by presenting an holistic scheme of things and therefore a presentation worth making.

This means that all reasonable models are viable. I am not making the mistake of suggesting that existing ones are wrong. They are just a different way of describing the same reality. If personal preference leads one to conclude that the Big Bang model of the universe is correct, then who am I to say it is not. It is another horse in the race and should not be discounted. But as a model, it has constraints as does the one I am describing but this model is much further reaching before its one major constraint is realised. A Constraint that I shall be identifying in order to show it to be as I say it is; the ultimate model of all creation and a constraint that we can use to show the face of first level existence reality[1].

[1]   *The constraint to which I am referring is that of passing through the single dimensional energy window, as I shall make clear in part three, chapter four, subheading "The constraint of the ultimate model".*

PART 3

THE UNIVERSE

Energy is the fourth dimension. All four make density. The universe must expand and in so doing goes into a four dimensional roll that provides a closed system that has no gaps in it. Such a shape has an edge and centre which are one and the same, with the centre passing through every point within it. This makes for an apparently infinite universe that is really finite.

CHAPTER 1
OVERVIEW TO PART THREE

Part three of the book will now present a model of the universe born of the three simple rules described in part two, chapter one, "Building Blocks". The rules were presented there as the basic principles behind a new universal theory. By now expanding them in the form of this overview, we can see - albeit only generally - an idea of where we have been, where we are going and what we are going to discuss in this part of the book.

1. *First there is existence* - *Second level existence in the form of our universe as perceived by us. There being no other way to perceive it because it IS by the act of perception.*

Part one addressed the issue of existence, there being two levels; one representing true reality, and the other being how that reality appears to us as its participants (see figure one on page 12). That apparent reality is what I have named as "second level existence" and is what part two of the book started to deal with.

I make the point now as I did then: the concept of first and second level existence is one that part one of the book cannot impart by itself. It is as we move to the heart of the theory, in which energy really starts to make its four dimensional presence felt, that the blur of first level existence will start to come into sharper focus.

Part two was slipped in between this and part one only to make obvious these very simple rules and, to show how obvious and simple rules can be: the first three dimensions are really one; time is not the fourth contender and; there must be another lurking about to facilitate a universe that curves in on itself, something the first three can't manage by themselves.

Certainly these arguments, in isolation, are not proofs in themselves but this is an holistic theory and by entering part three we will see how they start to "hang together" by taking a glimpse at a larger part of the overall-scheme-of-things. An expansion of the second rule will give us a summary of what is to be expected before reaching part four.

2. *Second there is movement - This is four dimensional movement (expansion), with energy being the fourth dimension which is expanding to provide a second level existence universe that curves in on itself by virtue of its own existence. Everything (including matter) is continually expanding infinitum. This then manifests itself as not only an apparently three dimensional infinity, but also a four dimensional finite shape which is closed, apparently fluid, and has no 'gaps', therefore able to accommodate gravity by the formation of matter within it.*

The formation of matter is a subject that will be covered in part four as will gravity but I include it here because it is relevant to the last of the three simple rules and, as always, allows a continuous view of where we are going.

3. *Then there is everything as a result of the first two - This is the result of differing rates of expansion within the universe, making itself apparent in the form of matter. The formation and interaction of this matter then creates, quite literally, everything.....* (the subject of part four).

The use of logical rules to construct a model of the universe

I propose that it should be permissible to use these three simple rules, and other such logical rules, to construct a model of the universe, for the equally simple reason that the Greater Intelligence 'thinks' logically. All of creation, part of which we witness, is the intellectual process of the

The Ultimate Explanation

Greater Intelligence. Given that it is a logical, rational, thinking (although not in the sense we would 'think') phenomena, then you would fully expect the second level existence universe, (that which is perceived by us as being what we think is true reality) to be nothing short of logical and rational especially as the Greater Intelligence and the universe are one and the same.

CHAPTER 2

ENERGY: THE FOURTH

DIMENSION

Overview

This chapter will explain how the first three dimensions account for volume, and how the fourth accounts for the energy that makes up that volume. All four dimensions being a function of volume and energy together. Energy is what gives volume a density. It will be explained how these four dimensions are responsible for the universe in which we find ourselves by placing energy into context along side the other three dimensions. This will show how the fundamental nature of energy is such that if anyone of the four dimensions are removed, it and the other three cease to exist. Thus extending the same rationale as described in part two, chapter two, "Three Dimensions" applying it to four dimensions instead of just three. Various thought experiments will be used to explain and demonstrate this.

Volume to density

In part two, chapter two, "Three Dimensions" argued that they are in fact one dimension in the form of volume. I also warned that I will go on to state that these three are three quarters of one dimension with energy forming the fourth quarter. This is quite so and nothing but obvious as we shall now see:

If a solid object is composed of height, width and depth - those three loveable characters that tantalise our common sense by being three separate quantities of

71

measurement that are totally inseparable (and therefore ultimately one) - then what happens if this three dimensional
object has more material in it than another of precisely the
same dimensions.

In other words; two solid cubes, both the same size
but one has more material in it then the other, i.e. it's more
dense than the other. What of the three dimensions high-
lights the fact that both are not the same in all respects?

The additional material, in one of the cubes, is going
to be somewhat disgruntled to think it makes no difference
to the rest of the universe whether it is there in great quantity or not. "Just a minute," it argues, "I might point out that
by being rarefied in my population, I get to call myself a
gas. And by being densely populated, I get the equally
grand title of being a solid. Surly that must count for
something. Can this not be offered up as an application for
a medal of dimensional recognition. It seams to me that my
density very much effects the status of the object that I
form. An object of which the other three dimensions only
serve to size. I mean, I know I am only an inanimate object
and therefore incapable of communication and thought
but..." at which point, sadly, its plea for recognition evaporates along with its confession of not being able to make the
plea in the first place. But we listened for long enough.
What we are talking about is the amount of energy gone
into making the mass within an object.

Einstein said that mass is energy and energy is mass.
They are one and the same. It must therefore be the case
that by gathering a lot of energy into one three dimensional
location, we find a solid object. Gather in only a small
amount and we find a gas. Any variation in between produces objects with varying densities.

So the missing element-of-description that differenti-
ates the two cubes is energy, or mass, which ever you
prefer to call it (I'm going to stick with "energy"). It provides the fourth quarter: height, width and depth gives us

volume - the first three quarters - and the amount of energy squashed into, and thereby forming that volume, gives us density - the final quarter: the fourth dimension.

Density

$$\text{Density} = \frac{\text{mass}}{\text{volume}}$$

Density is mass per unit volume. Mass is energy so we can also say that density is energy per unit volume. Unit means one, or the whole of. So we are talking about a variable amount of energy for any one particular size of volume.

If energy is the fourth dimension, how then does this compare with the other three? We established in part two that they are collectively one because they are joined by a seamless joint to make a volume. By removing one, they all disappear. So it is with energy. Remove energy (mass) and you can see how there is nothing left to which three dimensions can apply.

Against this, it could be argued that a three dimensional "frame" would be left but this would drag-up the base argument made in part two: to remove height is also to remove depth and width. And so it is with energy. Remove it and the three dimensional "frame" (height, width and depth) will also disappear because it needs to be made of something i.e. mass, which is energy. So by removing any one of the now *four* dimensions, the other three cease to exist.

This is all apart from the theoretical approach: the text book description that serves to explain it. By simply using the word "frame," within the above explanation, I have implied that three dimensions can exist separately from four. This is not the case in the real world but it is necessary, in theory, to fragment the solid object of density into four items of measurement in order to describe density in the first place. But that is all I'm doing by way of four separate

73

dimensions - *describing* it. This is in just the same way that, in part two, we discussed how it was feasible and necessary to fragment the single dimension of volume into three for the purpose of education: to impart the concept of height, width and depth. We went on to say that this was only in theory and could never be the case in real-world practice.

The three existing dimensions go to make volume and our new four dimensions make density. You cannot have density without creating volume. Volume is created by the act of gathering energy together to form a density. So the one real world dimension that we thought was volume is in fact density.

By now you will see that I have not come up with anything new. Density is as old as the hills, as is volume. What I am doing is stating the obvious and the only tools I am using is simplicity, logic and reason. Energy has to be the fourth dimension because without it the other three would disappear. They interact; they are interlocked; they are one and the same. I cannot say so much for time. If time were to disappear, volume would be totally unscathed. The consequences of the removal of time would be no more than leaving your watch at home. With no indication of time you would have to eat when you were hungry and not when you knew it was twelve thirty, but you would certainly not cease to exist. (Sorry. That was an unnecessary poke at "the time camp." If it works well for them then they should keep it. But for me it rattles around like a dry unnecessary pea in my "four dimensional camp" of density).

CHAPTER 3

THE EXPANDING UNIVERSE

Overview

This chapter will start to describe the second level existence four dimensional universe which is the universe as
perceived by us. It will describe a model of a model (see
figure one on page 12). The universe as perceived by us is
the ultimate model. It will model this model by presenting a
universe void of matter in the form of an expanding 'soup'
of 'smooth' energy. This will leave us with a conundrum by
describing a universe that expands until it folds in on itself.
The conundrum is that by expanding to the stage of folding
in on itself it must first have a boundary formed by nothing
and this is not possible because there is no such thing as
nothing as described in part two, "Space and the Need for a
Fourth Dimension." We shall return to this conundrum in
part five.

This chapter (as will the remainder of part three) will
ignore this conundrum. It will explain how the universe
came into existence by the act of expanding energy and
how that same expansion causes energy to then 'roll-off the
edge' of the second level existence universe.

First, the back ground to how astronomists know the
universe is expanding:

How do we know the universe is expanding?

For those that read a lot of scientific material, I suggest you
skip the next bit. It is just a regurgitation of the "whistling
train" to highlight the 'eey-aw' effect of the Doppler shift
and how that can be likened to the red shift in light. This in

turn reveals galaxies to be rushing apart - the widely accepted conventional belief that the universe *is* expanding.

As a train rushes towards you, its whistle sounds higher pitched than when it rushes away. The whistle produces sound waves one after the other at a steady rate. These travel to your ear as waves of pressure fronts arriving, as you would expect, one after the other. They vibrate your ear drum in sympathy and say "look out, here comes a train!" Rather like whipping up the end of a long rope laid on the ground: a wave travels along to the other end. Do it regularly and they arrive at the other end with the same regularity as you despatch them. Someone at the other end would count the waves as arriving with the same regularity.

But, if he was to run along beside the rope towards you, he would argue that they past his eye with an increased frequency compared to the rate at which you produced them. Likewise, if he stood still and you somehow slid the ground towards him, along with the rope, he would argue the same state of affairs. You've guessed the rest; the train is rushing towards you despatching the sound waves at a steady rate but your lug cops for them at a faster rate because its moving towards you. The faster it moves, the higher the pitch you hear because the pressure fronts are arriving at a faster rate. As the train rushes away from you, the pitch of the whistle lowers for the opposite reason.

Broadly speaking, light behaves like this. The light from a source arrives like waves, impacting upon your eye and telling you that the source is there. If it rushes towards you, the frequency of the light goes up. Away, and it goes down. The faster it moves away, the lower the frequency. So you can judge the speed at which the source is moving from you by how much the light frequency is reduced.

In the 1920s a gentleman by the name of Edwin Hubble set about looking at all the galaxies and noticed from the shift in light coming from them, that they were nearly all rushing away. (This shift displaces light towards the red end of the spectrum and so is called the "red shift". Needless to say; the naked eye could not see it). Those galaxies close by were measured to be heading off at a slower rate than those further away. In fact, the speed at which they were measured to be moving away, increased in direct proportion with their distance from us. He published his findings in 1929. The conclusion was drawn that if everything is rushing away from everything else, the bits that are rushing away must be sat in something which is expanding. The "something" in which they are sat is what is called "empty space" - nothing.

So there we have, in its broadest terms, the modern concept of an expanding universe - which also forms the back bone of the Big Bang theory. Although, I must say, it is interesting how "nothing" can be considered as existing, let alone expanding. Within the confines of the Big Bang theory, I have no problem with this, but within this theory, it has no place. If something is expanding such as to push the bits in it further apart like currents in an expanding dough in a baker's oven, then there must be something there to be doing the pushing. Take the dough away and you are left with a heap of currents sitting on the oven floor discussing the extremely hot weather they are having, and not the least bit interested in moving away from each other.

Energy as the prime mover

Energy cannot exist as a single dimension in the second level existence form. In this sense, it has no extension. A 'point,' to use Particle Physicist parlance, with no three dimensional extension. In order to manifest itself in the second level existence form, energy needs to extend out in three directions to form a four dimensional shape complete with density. The largest four dimensional shape in existence is that of the universe itself which would seem to have come into existence by the act of expansion.

The Ultimate Explanation

That is; energy - as a single dimension - creates the other three dimensions of volume in the form of the universe coming into existence by the act of expansion from a single dimension to that of three dimensions of volume. Volume being made up of energy with which to form the four dimensions of density.

Now, as we have said before, mass is energy and energy is mass. This comes from Einstein's famous equation: $E = mc^2$ This quite simply says that the (E)nergy, that goes into making up an object, is equal to its (**m**)ass times the speed of light (**c**) (186,000 miles per second) squared (^{2}). Given that "Squared" is the speed of light times the speed of light, you can imagine that we are talking about quite a bit of energy going into making any one object, no matter how small. The speed of light is always measured to be the same so when it comes to appreciating how much energy has gone into making an object, it's the mass that counts. The speed of light is used for scaling up whatever number represents the mass so that we can refer to it as energy.

Given that mass and energy are the same thing then, as we have already said:

$$\text{If density} = \frac{\text{mass}}{\text{volume}}$$

$$\text{and energy} = \text{mass}$$

$$\text{then density} = \frac{\text{energy}}{\text{volume}}$$

And what's more, as we have also just said, the universe would appear to have come into existence by the act of expanding. From this we can therefore deduce that it did so at the expense of energy. That is; energy constantly reducing in energy level to provide for an ever increasing volume - the expanding universe.

Part 3: The Universe

This we can deduce because when considering the universe coming into existence by the act of expanding energy, we can be sure that it had no boundary in order to confine the energy in the first place. We can be sure of this because in talking about the universe we are talking about all that exists so there can't be anything else with which to form a boundary and it certainly could not be formed by nothing. If this reducing energy level is unbound then it cannot help but expand into three dimensions of volume. If it did not expand into volume then the energy level could not drop.

And now enter the first glimpse of first level existence reality as we ask the question why should the energy want to drop in the first place? The answer is that the Greater Intelligence needs to manipulate energy in the only way possible to it and that is via its energy level. It needs to manipulate energy to 'think' because it *is* energy and thinking is what it does. We shall return to this rather bizarre statement in part five where we shall see why the level of energy is the only form of manipulation open to it. I shall tuck back my "winning ticket" for now and return to what we normally refer to as the 'real' world, that is in truth, second level existence.

To return to the subject of volumes, energy levels and the expanding universe; a good analogy would be to imagine a rectangle made of matches, first glued at their ends and then placed onto a sheet of rubber which is being stretched in all directions. The rubber represents the energy of an expanding universe. As it is stretched you will see the rubber in the rectangle as continuously reducing in density (a location of reducing density). If then you remove the matches and draw a square onto the rubber sheet and start it stretching again, the square will grow but the amount of the rubber within that square will always remain constant.

Therefore, it can be said that the universe has come into existence by virtue of all the locations within it being locations of expanding volume, expanding into an increasingly larger volume by virtue of every location within it being a location of reducing density. The reducing density in question is the density of energy. In other words, it is reducing-energy which is the *prime mover* which *then* causes volume to exist in an ever expanding fashion. It is not the increase in volume that primarily drives it to expand - it is the ever reducing energy that constitutes that volume. Returning to the rubber sheet analogy, in the context of energy being the prime mover, it is not the sheet being stretched that causes it to expand but the effect of the density-of-rubber-per-unit-area reducing at every location within the sheet, which *then* causes it to expand (with rubber representing energy). A bit like laying it on a hot plate and watching it melt into an expanded version of its former self rather than trying to stretch it by hand.

Energy *has* to be the prime mover. If volume were the prime mover, we would have to ask what it is that forms the device/system/mechanism that stretches the volume to form the universe and who made it, where did it come from and does it have a portable phone, the questions are limitless. But by considering energy as the prime mover, we only need concern ourselves with its nature and why it should reduce in level to cause the creation and subsequent expansion of the three dimensions of volume to form the universe. These questions are answered in part five but for now it gives us a picture of an expanding universe and the prime mover behind its expansion.

The four dimensional roll

It can now be said that the energy expands out in three dimensions at every location within the four dimensional density it is forming (the universe). The rate of expansion is equal at each location with "location" meaning each, every and any amount of energy within the system which is expanding from a single dimensional **point** into a three dimensional volume. It can be described as a **point** (before expansion) because it has no volumetric extension.

So much for the locations of energy within the whole but what about the whole that all these locations go to form, i.e. the universe. The outer most extension of the universe must be experiencing a faster rate of reduction in density because it is driven by a factor of all the other locations-of-reducing-density working together. This is because as any single point location expands to form a volumetric expansion of space, that newly formed space is itself a region in which more single point locations are coming into existence and themselves expanding - each expanding at the same rate. It is important to appreciate this because without it the outer most extension will not expand faster then the rest. This is all as a result of energy being the prime mover.

Eventually this outer most extension is driven through zero density, in advance of the rest of the whole, by the act of expansion. And zero density means zero energy. It has effectively 'rolled off the edge' of the universe. At this point it has no energy and therefore no volume. But the energy that once constituted the outer most extension, in tune with conventional belief, cannot be destroyed, only relocated and this is precisely what happens.

All the other locations within the whole are still reducing in energy level (locations of reducing density) because they are expanding. They therefore have an increasing energy demand. This energy demand is partially satisfied by the available energy which has 'rolled-off' from the outer most extension of the universe, being taken up and converted back into four dimensions by the act of expansion within the whole, instantly and at every location[1]: a 'four dimensional roll'.

---

[1]   *The fact that this transmission of energy is instan-*

It can be seen that the areas of increased energy demand, within the whole, always have a demand greater
than that which can be supplied by the energy which has
'rolled-off the edge'. This gives us a universe that, at any
location within it, is seen to be receiving a continuous low
level input of energy. Although it will not be clear in what I
have said so far, book two will show that this forms the
basis of what we interpret as the background microwave
radiation, supposedly the remnant of "The Big Bang."
Which in effect it is because it is as a direct result of expansion. (There is much more to be appreciated about this aspect of radiation. It falls within the category of
movement-within-the-universe, under the heading of the
True Nature of Light and that is dealt with in the next
book).

Four dimensional movement

The expansion that we are talking about is four dimensional
movement because the energy is expanding simultaneously
in three dimensions at the same time, all under the influence of reducing energy level. If energy level is falling then
the density must be falling, and density is four dimensional.
Therefore it must be four dimensional movement.

Three dimensional movement, considered separately
of energy level, is simply the act of a body travelling; moving from one location to another; whizzing about. Although
in parts four and five we will see how, in the universe, it is
not possible to move three dimensionally without the volume of a body being influenced under the force of gravity
and thereby demonstrating that really there is only one
form of movement and that is four dimensional. But it is
useful to consider the two as being separate *in theory*.

*taneous and at every location is explained and justified in
part five, chapter one, subheading "The primary cause of
expansion".*

Closed system

The point about the imbalance of energy rolling off the edge of the universe when compared to that required by the energy demand of all the expanding areas within it, is an important one. It further demonstrates how this constitutes a closed system. As described in the earlier explanation of a closed system, in part two, chapter three, subheading "A closed system with no gaps" - any disturbance in such a system will have an effect throughout the whole.

To see how this applies to our four dimensional roll, try to imagine an area of expanding energy as having its rate of expansion retarded in comparison to the rest. The rest would feel as though some of its volume had been reduced because the retarded area would appear to have condensed compared to the rest. This means that the three dimensional outer most extension of the universe would be smaller because the 'rolling-off energy' would reach zero density that much sooner: the effect of a disturbance (one area having a retarded rate of expansion) is transmitted throughout the whole of the system.

CHAPTER 4
ENERGY AS A SINGLE
DIMENSION

Overview

In this chapter, the first level existence 'winning ticket' will again be waved by stating that energy is the medium by which the Greater Intelligence 'thinks' and therefore *is* the Greater Intelligence. Energy supports intelligence and as such, forms the building blocks for the second level existence universe; its thinking mechanism, thereby falling in line with part one of the book.

Further, this chapter will emphasise how the *first* level existence format of energy is the fundamental cause of the four dimensional *second* level existence universe that we perceive. It will describe, in more detail, what happens as energy 'rolls-off' and becomes a single dimension and how it re-manifests itself in the form of continued expansion at every location within the universe.

First, this rolling-off-the-edge effect will be shown to be the constraint that identifies our universe as being an ultimate model of reality and not reality itself as now follows.

The constraint of the ultimate model

The energy which has "rolled-off" the three dimensional edge of the universe, by the act of being expanded out to zero density and thereby losing its volume, returns to the single dimension of energy with no three dimensional constraints. It therefore no longer manifests itself in the second

84

level of existence which is what we perceive as the universe and what I am calling "the ultimate model" (see figure one on page 12).

Having been released from its volumetric constraints at the three dimensional edge of the universe, energy now becomes one-dimensional. We have effectively followed energy, on its journey of expansion, out of the model we call "the universe" - second level existence which describes first level existence in the only way we know; by way of our experiences - and into first level existence itself. We have explored the ultimate model of reality to its limit, and then beyond, finding ourselves facing true reality - which is first level existence.

At this point, things become difficult to describe in terms of our second level existence multidimensional language. As such, I can only describe first level existence in second level existence terms. That is, as **a single dimension of energy that is pure intelligence which occupies no three dimensional extension at all.** This may seem a peculiar statement but only because I am making it to fellow human beings that perceive themselves as living in a multidimensional universe (which is second level existence). Parts four and five will go on to describe this single dimensional phenomena at length but for now it is important to appreciate the transition from a multidimensional universe to that of a single dimensional phenomena that takes place at the edge of the universe. This is because that is where the constraint of the multidimensional universe lies (a constraint that makes it a model of reality and not reality itself -see also part one, chapter one, subheading "A model of reality") for the following reason.

The argument summarised in the overview to chapter two, "Energy: the Fourth Dimension," would seem to contradict the idea of energy expanding to the point of loosing its three dimensional constraints to then return to a single dimension. The argument there stated that by removing any one of the four dimensions, it and the other three would cease to exist. Like that, by removing the three dimensions of volume, you would expect the remaining fourth dimension of energy to cease to exist. But this is true only when considering the second level existence model that we call the universe and it was in the context of that model - the ultimate model - that chapter two, "Energy: the Fourth Dimension" was seeking to justify energy as the fourth dimension. And, as above, we have had to leave that model in order to explore first level existence, *for that very reason*: because energy cannot exist in the second level existence universe as a single dimension. This is then the constraint that makes the perceived universe a model and not reality.

It is tempting to say at this point that the universe is in that case, reality in itself. This would then mean that there are no constraints upon it, which means that energy cannot exist as a single dimension in any sense. Given that I have said that energy is pure intelligence, which is single dimensional, which is first level existence, then it might be construed that first level existence does not exist.

But this overlooks three things. Firstly, that first level existence is the Greater Intelligence and to remove it is to remove the 'why' behind all of creation; a purpose and definition of mind, intelligence, existence etc. etc.. Secondly, to declare the universe that we perceive as reality means that it must exist in some kind of physical form quite separate of the mind and we established the problems connected with proving that idea in part one. (Not that it can be disproved, but it can't be proved either. So it can't take precedence over any other proposed form of existence). And thirdly, this would then mean that there has to be an edge to the universe formed by a boundary of nothing, and there is no such thing as nothing! Unless, of course, I simply say that it warps in on itself by virtue of a phenomena for which I can only offer a name and some kind of metaphorical explanation or tautology. Like; it bends in on itself at the edge because the edge of the universe is made of particles called "bendy-in particles" that do just that - that's not to say such an explanation is wrong, only that it could go an awful lot further to being more correct (!). Besides, such an explanation would leave just a glib description of 'how' with no explanation as to 'why' as I will explain in the subchapter "How' without the 'why" in the next chapter.

It is now that the 'winning ticket' of part one of the book really comes into play.

This single dimension, that is pure intelligence, includes us, or rather, our *minds*, as part of its intelligence. We, being data processing sub-units (processing data by the act of being intelligent), collectively enable part of this Greater Intelligence's 'thinking' capability. The data we process is information entering our minds via (what we see as) our bodies. The processing of that data is our every day thoughts. It is here that the second level existence universe manifests itself - in our minds. Just because we think it exists four dimensionally does not mean it does so in a fashion which is somehow solid and separate from our minds, only that it appears to. And therefore that is how we describe it; as a four dimensional physical thing which, for all our intents and purposes, *is* real. Real in every sense (including the physical sense) simply because *the universe is what it is* and the word physical has no latitude of experience to tell us what is meant by it. So at the end of the day, we can truly say that the universe is everything it appears to be and at the same time, that "..within is where without lies" (see poem inside front cover).

We all see the same universe, and each other, because we are all part of the same Greater Intelligence. It follows logical, predictable rules because it is a logical, rational, thinking system of intelligence. Therefore, by describing the four dimensional universe (that we believe surrounds us), by use of logical, predictable rules (or laws, that we identify by our experiences amongst them in terms of the human study that we call Science), we are not describing true reality but rather, something that implies it. That is to say; a model of it, or rather; an "ultimate model" because it is the nearest description to true reality that there is (see figure one on page 12). This is a model of first level existence which is the Greater Intelligence of which our minds form part. Modelled, that is, by the second level existence universe which we *think* exists and from which energy has "rolled-off" once it has expanded out to zero density at the edge of our second level existence universe.

Now, as I have said before, once the fourth dimension of energy has lost its volumetric constraint (by rolling-off the edge of the universe) it becomes **instantaneously available** at each and every single **point** location within the second level existence universe for the purpose of volumetric re-expansion back into the universe again. I use the term "point" to mean a location with no volumetric extension, and "instantly available at every location" because it is a single dimension in the first level existence form (before the act of re-expansion) and the first level of existence has no three dimensional extension (a volume). The energy 'travels' through no distance, from the three dimensional edge of the universe, to be present at every location at the same time, because it has no distance through which to travel. It therefore 'travels' instantaneously. (I have to say "travel" because I am bound by my four dimensional, second level existence thoughts). This will be further justified and explained in part five, chapter one, "The Mind of Our Creator," Subchapter "The primary cause of expansion".

CHAPTER 5
THE SINGLE DIMENSIONAL
ENERGY WINDOW

Overview

The foregoing chapter represents a peculiar concept but only because I am asking four dimensional eyes to view a one dimensional phenomena - that of first level existence (which is pure intelligence). When viewed from a second level existence four dimensional perspective only (without the use of first level existence) the phenomena can be equally described simply by use of something *called* a **single dimensional energy window**, giving a 'how' without bothering with a 'why' as follows:

'How' without the 'why'

Energy, having rolled-off the edge of the four dimensional universe by the act of expansion to zero density in advance of the rest of the whole, passes through what could be termed as a single dimensional energy window to become instantly apparent at every location within the universe in the form of continued expansion from within. That is an edge and centre which are one and the same (because they are separated by a window with no volumetric dimensions) with the centre passing through every point location within the universe.

In providing a how without the why, all I have just said is that the edge and centre are connected by something with no volumetric dimensions *called* "a single dimensional energy window" - a simple name, in other words. To then go on and enhance the window with something more tangible then just a name (i.e. an explanation of what the window is), is then to put a 'why' to the 'how'. This is exactly what an understanding of first level existence does. More on this in part five.

With or without first level existence, the result is exactly the same - the edge and centre are one and the same with the centre passing through every point within. First level existence only supplies the 'why'. It can be ignored but this leaves us with just a glib 'how' at the second level existence. The reason I am bothering to point out that the single dimensional energy window can be taken with or without the 'side salad' of a proper explanation is because it demonstrates how the 'how' can be left intact even if the first level existence concept is disengaged due to being misunderstood or unacceptable at this stage. This is the case for the entirety of the first level existence element of this theory (which will extend well past this first book alone). But, above all, it has to be said that the 'why' is far more important than the 'how' because to know why is to then realise how.

The infinite/finite expanding universe

What we have is an expanding universe which is three dimensionally *infinite* (going on forever) but which is also four dimensionally *finite* (not going on forever but having a set size to which there are limits to its extensions). "Finite" because, by realising the true four dimensions, we are able to realise a four dimensional edge (and centre) that provides for a universe that 'rolls in on itself' to continue expanding from within. "Infinite" because, by realising only three dimensions, it *appears* to expand out forever in the form of an infinite extension or linear infinity.

The closed, finite universe

By viewing the universe through four dimensional eyes (with energy as the fourth dimension) we see a finite shape that facilitates a closed system because it rolls in on itself in the form of a closed infinity. This is a closed system in which no gaps can exist because, as explained in part two, chapter three, "Space and the Need for a Fourth Dimension," there is no such thing as nothing with which to form a gap. And it is in a closed system with no gaps that Einstein's and Newton's theory of gravity can be exactly accommodated as will be described in part four: Gravity, Matter and Mass.

The Three dimensionally infinite universe

I will now briefly reiterate the concept of the universe appearing to have an infinite extension: stretching on forever. This is important because this is how most people envisage it to be.

The basis of the idea being: if you imagine yourself as being any one particular area of expanding volume of energy, your centre will move apart from all the other areas of expanding volume by the act of expansion. Finally you will find yourself at the 'edge' of the four dimensional universe, at which point you will 'roll-off' by virtue of loosing your volumetric extensions, passing through the single dimensional energy window to elute instantaneously from every point within the universe. The same universe from which you have just rolled-off, eluting from within it in the form of continued expansion.

Fine, this we have said before, but the point that should not be missed here is that you would not realise any transformation from being a three dimensional volumetric expansion to that of a single dimension of energy and back to a volumetric expansion again, because the energy window, through which you have travelled, has no three

91

dimensional extension and therefore no length through which to travel. It provides a seamless joint between the largest thing in the universe (the full extension of the universe itself) and the smallest (the fundamental, single point locations throughout the universe from which energy expands into volume and density).

This being the case, you would notice no change in your circumstances. As far as you are concerned, you have simply continued to expand. What you can see by way of your environment would also appear unchanged because you can look both ways through the window. In short, if you are blissfully unaware of the true forth dimension of energy and its true nature, you would consider, from a three dimensional point of view only, that the universe simply stretches on forever, you and it expanding infinitum. If you could travel in a 'straight' line in a universe otherwise void of three dimensional movement (whizzing about) you would expect to 'roll up' past your starting point having past through the seamless joint formed by the single dimensional energy window.

CHAPTER 6
MICROSCOPIC UNIVERSE

The exploration of what happens after passing through the single dimensional energy window at the edge of the universe, and the nature of this window, constitutes a complete explanation of the fundamental structure of matter and its behaviour. Atoms and their constituency, in other words. This is very much part of this theory but one that would produce a book the same size as this.

Given that it can be neatly categorised as being outside of the macroscopic universe (from a conventional three dimensional point of view that is), the microscopic universe will form the subject of book three. This will further justify and explain the apparently bizarre statement that the edge of the universe passes through the centre which is at each and every location within the universe, and further, that the *same* universe lies at each centre point. This gives rise to a fascinating situation that should appeal to science fiction readers. It means that within each and every particle, lies each and every *other* particle; any one object is contained within in any other; and any object is contained within itself. We will travel on a four dimensional microscopic journey into an object in book three using just three vehicles; imagination, logic and reason, to show that science fiction is not required to realise the four dimensional mechanics involved. Book three will also explain how matter passes through the energy window.

As mentioned in the above chapter; there is a question of 'looking' through the energy window. This involves the realisation of the true nature of light, which, in itself is part of a complete description of movement. This will form the subject of book two. The act of moving through the window will also be explained, analysed and justified as part of an overall scope that explains three dimensional movement (as opposed to four dimensional movement) and all its derivatives in the universe.

For now, the purpose is to lay the groundwork for this single holistic theory by concentrating on an explanation of the macroscopic universe along with its purpose and the mechanics involved, all of which can be derived by examining four dimensional movement. To that end we will now return to the driving force behind it.

CHAPTER 7

WHY THE UNIVERSE IS
EXPANDING AND NOT
CONTRACTING OR STATIC

We have thus far established that the universe goes into a four dimensional roll and continues to do so infinitum with continued expansion. By the Greater Intelligence sustaining the presence of energy in the second level existence form, energy cannot help but perform this four dimensional roll. This is why the universe is expanding and what's more, why it is expanding and not contracting. If it were to contract, it would return to a single dimension with no extension, and the other three dimensions (and therefore the second level existence universe) could not exist. The first level existence intelligence would not be able to 'think' (process data) and this is the sole purpose of the universe.

It is also not possible for the universe to expand to a finite limit and stop because the edge would have to be formed by a boundary of nothing and nothing cannot exist, as explained in part two, chapter three, "Space and the Need for a Fourth Dimension." (remembering that we are ignoring this constraint when considering a universe that has to expand before it reaches the point of a four dimensional roll. This will be addressed in part five).

Besides, as I have already said, the Greater Intelligence needs to expand energy into four dimensions in order to process data (to be explained in more detail in parts four and five). Although, in the true nature of things, the Greater Intelligence, as single dimensional energy in the first level of existence, does not really expand energy to form four dimensions. This is simply the way we see it from our blissfully ignorant second level existence universe point of view, even though we, in the form of our minds, are actually part of the first level existence. When modelling first level existence by use of our second level of existence universe, we see it as having to expand from a single dimension, with no extension, to that of a three dimensional volume complete with energy to form the four dimensional density of the universe. This is because this is the only way we can understand it.

This means that in true-nature, first level existence terms, the four dimensional, 'physical' universe, that we see around us, is in fact a model that describes the 'thinking' process of the Greater Intelligence. We are 'seeing' the mind of the Greater Intelligence, if you like. If this is a model of its thinking process, then it needs to have expanded it to achieve what the model looks like. And, given that any thinking process is an ongoing (or dynamic) process then it needs to continually expand to support continuous 'thought'.

What we have now envisaged is an expanding universe that is expanding in order to facilitate the thought processes of a Greater Intelligence. But it is a universe void of what we see as matter and it is the creation and interaction of this matter that truly provides for its intricate thought processes. Therefore, what we have envisaged is only its consciousness, in the form of an expanding universe created from 'smooth' energy, suitable for (although not actually) data processing which is supported by continuous consciousness.

CHAPTER 8
RECAP TO PART THREE

To summarise the nature of this energy and the way in which it expands in the second level existence universe, let me offer this. Its expansion is not due to the first level existence Greater Intelligence pumping energy into an otherwise empty black universe like air into a balloon. This energy *is* the universe, and *is* the first level of existence intelligence, carrying out its thought processes in the form of four dimensional second level existence which we see as the universe. Each and every part of its energy constituency is seen as expanding by us (by virtue of the Greater Intelligence's thinking process). It is not subject to the continuous input of additional energy. It only has a finite amount of energy with which to expand.

CHAPTER 9
THE SHAPE OF THE UNIVERSE

This sort of shape could never be viewed from the outside, only from within. There is no escape. To view from the outside requires some device / physical presence / manifestation of energy to facilitate the viewing, constituting additional discrete energy. For this discrete energy to exist separately of the whole would require a separation consisting of nothing and nothing cannot exist.

It could not be viewed properly from within either. Because from the edge to everything between it and the centre (present at every location within the universe) is connected by the instantaneous transmission of energy through a single dimensional energy window. It therefore appears to stretch on forever because the edge and centre are one and the same, connected by a seamless single dimensional joint.

PART 4

GRAVITY, MATTER & MASS

The whole universe is expanding energy. Matter is also expanding energy. A body of matter is formed by a quantity of energy expanding at a slower rate than that of its surroundings. This retarded rate of expansion produces a force that diminishes by the inverse square of the distance from the centre: a gravitational field. This force interacts between bodies of matter to provide an attraction in accordance with Newton's universal law of gravitation. The mass of any body of matter is effected by the gravitational field produced by other bodies of matter. The Greater Intelligence is responsible for the formation of matter as an input to its thinking mechanism that we call the universe. This also accounts for the universal forces at work in the universe.

CHAPTER 1
OVERVIEW TO PART FOUR

Don't worry about trying to understand the contents of this overview. I shall simply list the facts, as I see them, in their broadest terms, no matter how outlandish they may seem, and then revisit each item by way of an explanation as we chug through part four.

- If you envisage one area of the expanding energy, within the whole (the whole that constitutes the expanding universe, hitherto void of matter as described in part three) and retard its rate of expansion with respect to the rest, you have an area of increased energy with respect to its surroundings. This appears as a condensed particle - the formation of matter.
- If you look at the area around this retarded expanding area, you would see a gradually reducing energy level as you observe further from the retarded area, with the energy level reducing until it becomes equal to the rest of the universe. As you observe outwards, the change in energy level (compared to that which prevailed before the area was retarded) would reduce by the square of the distance as measured from the centre of the retarded expanding area. In other words:-

by the ratio $\dfrac{1}{d^2}$ a gravitational field.

- If you create two such retarded expanding areas, their gravitational forces would try to draw them together by the ratio of their two masses multiplied together and

100

divided by the square of the distance between the two centres:-

$$\frac{m \times m}{d^2}$$ which is Newton's law of universal gravitation.

(Construction has started in order to facilitate the Greater Intelligence's thought patterns).

• Create a multitude of retarded areas, to varying degrees, and allow three dimensional movement (with respect to their centre points) as a result of gravitational influence, and everything in the universe can be constructed - The universe as we see it becomes apparent: the Greater Intelligence is 'thinking'.

Although Rip'em smart-bottom Wesley would have had no problem with this, for the rest of us it has to be said that, although it might be of some interest, ultimately, its down right confusing. So what does it all mean? First a bit about the conventional theories of gravity:-

CHAPTER 2

CONVENTIONAL THEORIES OF

GRAVITY

Sir Isaac Newton, in 1687, came up with what he called his **law of universal gravitation** which states that the gravitational attraction between any two objects in the universe is proportional to the product of the masses divided by the square of the distance between them.

Put in mathematical talk: gravity is proportional to $\dfrac{m \times m}{d^2}$

    The inverse square, that the denominator 'd^2' represents, is what holds the planets of our solar system in an elliptical orbit around the Sun. In fact the whole equation goes to predict their orbits very accurately. Newton referred to this as **a force at a distance** but could not identify the support structure that transmits this force through space. Then along came Einstein with his Theory of Relativity. This took the form of two parts: Special Relativity and General Relativity. The first was published in 1905 and the second in 1915. General Relativity embodies an explanation of gravity which, for the most part, endorses Newton's equation but Einstein concerned himself not with the "force acting at a distance" but the way in which space and time is deformed by having massive bodies sitting within it. Rather like a mattress being deformed by having a heavy lead ball sitting on it. The idea being that this deformation of space and time (or "warping" as it is often called) then effects the natural path of those massive bodies and all without the need of any kind of force as offered by Newton. This means that their paths are influenced in such a way as to

Part 4: Gravity, Matter and Mass

only *appear* as though a "force acting at a distance" was at work. By this I mean that on one hand we have the Einstein school of gravity, with two lead balls rolling towards each other because of the deformation of the mattress upon which they sit (two dimensionally speaking), and the Newton school of gravity on the other hand, whereby they move together simply because they are joined by a stretched elastic band (the force acting at a distance) with the deformity of the surface upon which they sit, playing no part. Despite all that, Einstein, like Newton, could not tell us what it was that was being deformed by the bodies other than to call it space and time (or "spacetime" as some would argue).

Einstein's version can almost be regarded as a photographic negative of Newton's, except that Einstein's view of things revealed a discrepancy between the two theories with his version being generally agreed as matching observation. The discrepancy was that of the **precession of Mercury's perihelion** - Einstein's theory accommodates it, Newton's does not.

Mercury follows an elliptical orbit around the Sun but the Sun is not at the centre of this orbit. It is offset to one end such that as Mercury travels into that end of its orbit, it draws closer to the Sun. This point of closest approach is called its perihelion and this point slowly rotates around the Sun over the period of many years. Rather like squashing a hoop into an elliptical shape and swinging it around your finger. Your finger is the Sun and the point of contact with the hoop is the perihelion of Mercury's orbit. This point of contact moves around the surface of the finger which is equivalent to the precession of the perihelion. All rather loosely related but it gives you the general picture. We will return to this later but the point for now is that Einstein's theory predicts this precession where as Newton's does not.

The difference between the two theories is small, to say the least, but becomes most pronounced with Mercury because it is the planet that draws closest to the Sun and the

The Ultimate Explanation

Sun is the most massive object in our solar system. This difference between the theories is extremely subtle and diminishes yet further as we observe the movement of planets at a greater distance from the Sun. The difference between Newton's universal law of gravitation and that of Einstein's are virtually indistinguishable with these planets that lay further out. Newton's "$m \times m/d^2$" is the equation offered within most walks of education and one that I shall use for the following purpose:-

Having described what I believe to be the shape, structure and purpose of the universe in the preceding parts, in terms of a universe with no matter in it, I now need to anchor that system to observation. I will show that if matter forms within in it, in the way that I shall describe in this part of the book, such a system cannot help but produce the effect of gravity as we observe gravity to take place in the universe that we perceive as surrounding us. This gives the theory observational credibility as well as providing an explanation for what transmits gravity through so called empty space, not to mention an account of precisely what matter is.

I am, by way of this book, laying the base case, the broad support structure for the overall scheme of things; a qualitative description not a quantitative one. That will follow in the form of the subsequent books in this series that will eventually disclose the entire theory. For now I am drawing a simplistic macroscopic picture of the nuts, bolts and hinges of a unified theory. I am not detailing their thread-rates, lengths and diameters and to that end "$m \times m/d^2$" serves well to show that this is a base case that should be taken seriously, as opposed to delving into the very much more complicated 'photographic-negative' version of Einstein's. However, I will, within these pages, qualify how Einstein's and Newton's theories of gravity can be unified.

Part 4: Gravity, Matter and Mass

In case you are wondering how I can converge with Einstein's results when his theory includes a dependence on the warping (deforming) of time as a dimension, and I argue that time is *non*-dimensional, I would offer this: if Einstein's model includes time as a dimension, then time *does* indeed exist as a dimension and *does* warp. On the face of it, this may seem as a contradiction but can I refer you to "Philosophy of Theories" at the end of part one. From there it can be seen how I can make the statement that this model of creation does not displace Einstein's theory of Relativity. It is simply another model that happens to describe that same particular aspect of reality in which I have no use for time as a dimension - within the confines of this theory. Within the confines of Einstein's theory, time *is* dimensional. Both are viable and correct and should not be compared one to the other. The reality to which they both look is the only thing that should connect the two. (This is true for all theories that describe the same reality).

Time as in the ticking of a clock and the rotation of its hands: yes, a place of honour exists within this theory. But as a dimension: no. As the movement of hands, or indeed the movement within an atom to produce the same gradua-ted-movement effect as 'time,' 'time' within this theory can certainly be seen and measured to warp in the same way as it does in Einstein's. But I define time as being nothing more than movement and movement is already spoken for by way of the first three conventionally accepted dimensions of up/down, left/right, backward/forward. It is this three dimensional movement that warps to produce the same effect. But as "movement", the warping of time lies outside the scope of this book and within the next. I mention it now only so as to demonstrate that there is much still to come that, at first, it might seem I have overlooked.

CHAPTER 3

THE NON-EXPANDING UNIVERSE

First of all, let's get rid of all the expansion which has played a large part so far. It complicates things when, for the present, the expanding aspect is not needed. Let's look at the entire universe as being just as we envisage it to be; not expanding but stationary (or static).

By which I mean, I have so far described a universe which is composed of nothing but pure energy in a state of continuous expansion. I have not put any matter into it yet and that is what we are about to do in this part of the book. But when we do, you will see that it is not matter as we conventionally view it. It is matter that itself is continuously expanding, which means that once added, we have a universe in which quite literally *everything* is expanding. And I mean everything: you, me, the neighbour's cat, the planet; each and every piece of matter within the universe, as well as the universe itself. This is opposed to conventional belief whereby the space between astronomical bodies is the only thing that is considered to be expanding, with matter being in a state of not expanding. It may sound crazy but once the mechanism of this universal expansion is realised, we will not only see how matter is created and why it should ex- hibit the phenomenon that we call gravity but also why the continuous expansion of matter is indiscernible from a human point of view. But to get to that stage it is best to first view things as being in a state of non-expansion.

So like that, when we look at a collection of particles, we presently, and by convention, conclude them to be what we call "matter" which has been formed by a high con- centration of energy, as Einstein pointed out; $E = mc^2$. I in- terpret this as meaning that energy has somehow (explained later) gathered itself into a smaller volume of capacity. This is energy which has effectively been gathered in from the surrounding comparatively low-level-energy that we call space. Once gathered in, it appears to us as 'lumpy-bits': atoms; subatomic particles; particles; bodies; water; Mercury; oxygen; footballs; oranges; London Bridge; planets; stars; asteroids whatever we might care to call them once they manifest themselves as individuals or collectively.

Having formed, these lumpy bits then seem to just sit there. Other than interacting with each other, by virtue of three dimensional movement, they certainly don't seem to be expanding. This is a static view and one that I shall adopt to begin with. I shall also go one step further and make the assertion that the space between astronomical bodies is *not* expanding. This is all for the sake of explanation that I call a static model. And yes, you have guessed it - as a model it has constraints. These constraints will be identified to once again lead us back closer to the truth, that expansion is taking place at every corner of the universe. This expansional aspect will then take the form of a dynamic model that I will reintroduce later complete with expanding matter. For now we can get a handle on what is happening in the dynamic model by scrutinising the static model. A model-of-a-model, if you like - a submodel.

This later reintroduction of the concept of expanding space and matter, is where the true state of affairs will be revealed. Whereby, matter has not formed by condensed energy at all but is simply not expanding at the same rate as its surroundings (against which we take our reference). Its surroundings, and all of space, themselves expanding at faster rates even though matter *appears* to be condensed energy to us as participants of this model.

CHAPTER 4
GRAVITY IN A NON-EXPANDING UNIVERSE

Overview

In this chapter we will be able to see how it is that an astronomical body (such as the planet Earth) exhibits gravity as a result of being formed *from*, and being *in*, a closed, apparently fluid, four dimensional universe created from energy.

It will demonstrate the three dimensional mechanics of such an effect with the help of a piece of imaginary sponge, a two dimensional analogy with bubbles on the surface of water and a tank of water. The three dimensional mechanics being, quite simply, how an object is able to travel through any of the three dimensions of up/down, left-/right and backwards/forwards under the influence of gravity: bodies of matter being drawn together.

Sponge model

Imagine a large lump of sponge in the shape of a sphere. You now have yourself a model of the universe. The sponge material represents the energy that makes up the universe and given that it has no areas of anything other than continuous sponge, it is representative of a universe composed of pure smooth energy with no matter in it. The density is constant throughout its entirety.

Now imagine that a small spherical volume at the centre of that sponge is coloured red. Apart from its colour, the red sphere is exactly the same as the rest of the sponge with exactly the same density. While we've got the mental paint-pot out, colour the rest of the sponge blue.

Now condense the red sphere to say, half its original volume. Remembering that this is a thought experiment, the sphere can only condense under the force or 'clamp of our imagination'. This is now to represent the formation of matter by the concentration of energy into a smaller volume. The sphere is still composed of the same amount of sponge but occupies half the volume so its density has doubled. Its colour is still red but you can imagine it being somewhat more intense as the same amount of colour is concentrated into half the volume.

What has happened to the rest of the sponge? It is all joined; it is a continuum and cannot be separated. This is a system with no gaps in it so the surrounding material has no choice but to follow the walls of the red sphere in a direction towards the centre of the sphere until, that is, the walls stop at the new volumetric size of half that which it used to occupy.

Between the wall of the red sphere and the outer wall of the overall sponge shape, is deformed blue coloured material. As such, you would expect the shade of blue to reflect its newly deformed circumstances brought about under the influence of the red spherical section condensing. The different colours mark the difference between the sphere (red / matter / high level energy) and the surrounding sponge (blue / space / low level energy).

Given that all of the blue coloured sponge has followed the wall of the red coloured sphere inwards, including the outer wall of the overall sponge shape, the blue material must have increased in density throughout. It must therefore be said that the increased density is being held in a state of increased density by something. If it wasn't then it would spring back out to its original size and density. So what is holding it there? We know that the cause is that of the central sphere condensing but what is the mechanism that links the reduction of the central sphere to the increased density of the surrounding material? It doesn't just happen because "a little dickie bird told it to". It felt an unavoidable urge for its blue coloured constituent substance to gather closer together and remain in a state of increased density, as held by something.

That "something" would have to be a *force*. A force that emanates from the surface of the condensed red sphere and one that acts on the blue sponge in such a way as to maintain it in a newly concentrated form. (The removal of the force would allow the sponge to return to its original, less concentrated form as prevailed before the red sphere condensed). As you would expect, this force is constant as it 'radiates' out in three dimensions, making its presence felt in the form of sustaining the medium, through which it passes, in a state of higher concentration.

But, although the force remains constant, it is having to spread itself over an area of increasing size as it radiates out equally in all directions from the surface of the central sphere. And so the force, as measured along a radial line drawn from the centre of the red sphere to the wall of the overall sponge, would gradually diminish as it passes through the blue sponge. The way in which it diminishes is a function of the increasing size of sponge through which it travels and we know from geometry that the size would increase by the square of the distance from the centre. Therefore **the force diminishes by the inverse square of the distance as measured along the radial line.**

One way to see how geometry dictates such an increase in size is to view the blue sponge as being composed of spherical shells. Working our way out from the surface of the red sphere, we can say that the very thin layer of sponge that sits on that surface is the first shell. The next thin layer attached to the surface of that shell would be the second and so on. The size of each shell would have to be lager than the previous and the rate at which these shells become larger is known to be proportional to the square of the increase in distance that the radius of each shell represents. This is what I mean by saying that the blue sponge becomes larger as the force radiates out through it.

The way in which the force diminishes is much the same as the intensity of light: if you could flash a light bulb on and off quick enough, a thin spherical shell of light (often referred to as a **light-shell**) would travel out in all directions simultaneously. If you could then somehow freeze the light shortly after it has left the bulb, it would look like a spherical shell the surface of which would have a certain light intensity as measured at any one point upon it. Allow it to go on expanding into a shell of twice the diameter and freeze again. Measure the light intensity of that new larger size of shell at any one point on it and it would be four times less intense than previously. It is the same amount of light that is emanating out to form larger and larger areas of shells and therefore having to spread itself more and more thinly thus producing a light intensity which is less each time: proportionately less by the inverse square of the distance because this is the rate at which it has to spread itself more thinly.

Take any variation of this increasing size of shell set-up and you will see an inverse square law with respect to the intensity, and conversely; a square law with respect to its surface area (intensity goes down as the shell gets larger, and the surface area goes up). As laws go, this one is pretty universal to say the least. It is the result of three dimensional behaviour.

Tug

As I said towards the end of part one, there is always more than one way of looking at the same reality. As such we can now talk in terms of the two subtle faces of force, or equally; "tug:" The red sphere condenses and consequently "tugs" on the rest of the blue sponge. *Conversely*; the sphere condenses and the blue sponge tugs on *it*, trying to pull it back out to its original volume and reclaim its 'lost' material. The material that the blue sponge feels it has lost is the volume by which the red sphere has condensed. The consequential deformation of the blue sponge is the act of the sponge trying to do something about it. If it didn't, there would be no tug. Just as; if the red sphere did nothing about trying to retain its new condensed form, it would not tug back against the rest of the sponge. Both tugs are the same thing but viewed from two different angles.

Either way, a tug-effect is set up throughout the sponge which emanates from the surface of the red sphere. The total amount of tug coming from the sphere's surface is a set amount for a given degree of condensing by that sphere (if the sphere condensed more the tug would become greater). For a given degree of condensing, its total tug doesn't change as its effect radiates out through the blue sponge. But, like the light shell, it has to spread that same amount of tug through a larger and larger area as we look at shells of increasingly larger size with respect to the point of emanation. The **square** of the distance relationship means that a shell that has a radius of **twice** that measured from the centre to the first shell (the sponge immediately adjacent to the wall of the red sphere), has an area **four** times greater than the first shell. It therefore has a tug which is four times less at any one location on that shell when compared to a location on the first shell. The tug from the red sphere has four times the area through which to pull as it emanates through the larger shell. The overall effect is a reduction in size of the lump of spherical shaped sponge.

Closed system

As detailed in part two, chapter three, subheading "A closed system with no gaps," and part three, chapter three subheading "Closed system," a disturbance in such a system will be transmitted throughout the whole. We can see this effect, in the case of this sponge model, in the form of the disturbance generated by the act of the red sphere condensing. The disturbance is transmitted throughout the whole of the material to the point of causing a reduction in size of the overall shape.

Overall picture

Let's take a step back from this model and remind ourselves of the overall picture that it represents. The sponge is energy. The red sphere, once condensed, is energy that has condensed into a smaller volume of space to become what we call "matter," and the force that maintains the increase in density of the surrounding energy, as we range away from the surface of that matter, is following the inverse square law as measured from the centre. The whole point of the model is, of course, that gravity is observed to follow this same law. As you move away from the surface of matter, the gravity it exhibits drops off by the inverse square of the distance from the centre of that matter.

Field

But we are only *considering* the force placed upon the energy surrounding the matter and not its effect. By simply observing the change in force along a radial line drawn from the surface of that matter, we are not seeing it manifest itself in the way that you would expect gravity to. That is, by pulling things together. We are simply looking at the **field** that it generates. Generated by the act of energy condensing to form matter which thus becomes the origin of that gravitational field by virtue of being matter formed *in* and formed *from* a closed system of energy with no gaps in it. Such a system is provided as described in part three. We can't see it perform until it has something on which to perform and to see that we have to cause another piece of matter to form inside our sponge model.

Two spheres

To create another blob of matter in our sponge model we must start from scratch by having our piece of sponge contain two separate red spherical volumes of sponge, both of which then condense to half (or any fraction for that matter) of their original volume. The rest of the sponge is still coloured blue.

Each condensed sphere considered separately of the other would produce the same effect as the single condensed sphere previously described: the tug would emanate out from the surface and diminish by the inverse square of the distance. When considered together each would place a tug on the other and the tug each places on the other would diminish by this same ratio with respect to their distance apart. So it can be said that the attraction between them depends upon the inverse square of their distance apart (between centres) and the amount by which they have condensed.

Ratio of gravitational attraction

According to Newton's universal law of gravitation, the degree (or ratio) that any two objects attract each other by is proportional to $m \times m/d^2$. where 'm' is the mass of one of the objects and the other 'm' is the mass of the other object. The 'd' is the distance between the two objects. This gives us just as I have said; a proportion. If either or both of the masses increase then the magnitude of gravity between them goes up. Inversely, if the distance between the two objects increases, the magnitude of gravity between them goes down by the square of that distance: our much loved inverse square law.

Now, the mass of our two objects (the condensed red spheres) within the sponge, is represented by the amount of sponge (representing energy) that was originally selected, by the mental act of painting them red, in order to then squash them into a smaller volume. By the reckoning of the conventional understanding of what we call "mass," no matter how that volume is reduced, the mass remains the same because the amount of material within it is unchanged. But in my model we can see that the gravitational attraction between the two is dependent on a third variable, namely; the amount by which that amount of sponge (energy) has condensed. That is, if one of the spheres were to condense further, it would tug on the other that much more regardless of its distance from the other or the amount of energy gone into making either of them. Is this a constraint? In conventional terms; yes. But as we have seen before, these constraints lead the way to the true reality of things and this is no exception.

To see how, we need to ask the question; what do we mean by the word "mass?"

Mass

Einstein has told us that mass is energy ($E = mc^2$). Energy is required in large quantities before it manifests itself to man's instruments-of-measurement as having measurable mass. I would further argue that this happens when a large volume of energy is gathered into a smaller volume. When something is said to have mass it is then concluded that it is composed of matter. Mass is the conventional quantification of the amount of matter of which that something is composed. When Einstein pointed out that mass and energy are the same thing, he must also have meant that matter and energy are the same thing. That is, energy that has been gathered together in large quantities to manifest itself to our instruments-of-measurement as matter. This manifested

115

matter, which I interpret as being formed by the increase of energy level within a certain three dimensional locality, will exist four dimensionally because it has density.

To summarise:

Energy = mass (Einstein).

Matter = manifested mass (manifesting itself to our instruments-of-measurement).

So called "empty space" = unmanifested mass (Not manifesting itself to our instruments-of-measurement).

Energy = mass = matter

So, broadly; mass is energy and matter is also energy therefore matter, mass and energy are all the same thing. But logic is pulling on my shirt sleeve to insist that mass is not only the amount of energy contained within a certain volume but also the amount by which that energy has condensed to form that volume. The ratio, in other words, of the volume that originally contained the energy (V_1) compared to the volume to which that energy is then reduced (V_2) to manifest itself as having measurable mass. The greater the ratio, the grater the gravitational effect because its 'mass' is greater. This then preserves the equation $m \times m/d^2$ but lends a new definition to what is meant by "mass."

Lead ball experiment

Some time ago an ingenious experiment was performed which effectively amounted to a lead ball being suspended along side another fixed lead ball. The observed result was equivalent to the suspending wire being angled towards the fixed ball so as to describe the $m \times m/d^2$ relationship of gravity, thereby demonstrating that any and every piece of matter exhibits gravity by virtue of its mass. My assertion would then have it that if the fixed lead ball were to be somehow reduced to a proportion of its size, the other would be correspondingly more attracted toward it. This would indeed happen but to such a minute amount that it would be impossible to measure.

To see why, we need to remember that the amount of energy that goes into even the tiniest object is its mass times the enormous figure for the square of the speed of light, with the speed of light being 186,000 miles per second. If V_1/V_2 is correct, then V_1 must have been an enormous volume to encompass a sufficient amount of energy to then be reduced to V_2 to form the mass which constitutes the lead ball. A further reduction in the size of that ball would therefore have a proportionally minute effect.

Put another way: it is presently considered that space has little or no mass but just because our instruments-of-measurement might not detect mass (energy) does not mean that there is no energy (mass), only that it is low level energy which is not measurable as mass. (See also part two in which space and energy are seen to be the same thing. The question of the existence of an ether and its detection is addressed in part five). If so called empty space is referred to as such (because the energy, from which it is constructed, is so low as to be undetectable) then it must be so low as to require an enormous volume of it to be gathered together into a smaller volume before it can be detected as mass. Thus falling in line with my argument.

I would be worried if space were said to be made up of high level energy because that would mean V_1 need only be quite small and a small further reduction in the size of something like our lead ball would result in a measurable change in mass and that does not fit with observation (i.e. mass is measured to remain constant with reduction in volume). But this is not the case, V_1 would need to be very large. As such, the act of compressing the lead ball further is superficial to the point of being impossible to measure.

The other side to this coin is that as V_1 is reduced, for each equal amount of reduction in size you would expect the gravitational pull to increase by steps that become larger and larger: a non-linear relationship in other words. And given that the lead ball would be nearly as small as it can get, in relation to the gob-smackingly large volume from which it was reduced, a further reduction in size, no matter how slight, would be expected to produce an appreciable effect with respect to the gravity it exhibits.

But the lead ball is *not* nearly as small as it can get. In *theory*, the smallest the ball can get is to reduce to the point where it passes back through the single dimensional energy window, which, as bazaar as it may seem (and yet no more bizarre than the summary comments of the effect of Einstein's Relativity), makes it so small that it is as large as the whole universe. This is as described in part three and is in support of the logic of an apparently three dimensionally infinite universe that rolls in on itself to present a four dimensionally finite system. That four dimensionally finite system is one that is facilitated by a universe that is expanding and we are presently considering a universe that is not expanding. But let's break with that for a moment and reintroduce the aspect of expansion in which matter (the lead ball in this case) is formed by being energy which is not expanding as fast as its surroundings (as will be made more clear later). Like this we can get a clear view as to why passing back through the single dimensional energy window is theoretically possible and thereby demonstrating that the ball is nowhere near as small as it can get even compared with the enormous volume from which it originally condensed, but only in theory. In practice it would be impossible.

To get the ball to pass back through the single dimensional energy window would require us to compress it against the expansion of the universe and contract the ball in excess of its own rate of expansion. This would be like trying to run faster than a fast moving car: if it where possible to catch-up with the car, once neck and neck you are *not* moving relative to each other, to run even faster means you are then achieving your goal of running faster than the car. The expansion of the energy that forms the matter that we call "the lead ball" is the fast moving car and by us trying to perform the impossible task of compressing the ball at an equal and opposite rate to its expansion, only serves to give us a ball that is stationary relative to the rest of the expanding universe. To reach the goal of compressing it back through the window means we have to compress it even faster and that is simply not possible. That is not to say that passing through the window is not its smallest extent; as far as the universe and the ball is concerned, it is. It simply is not possible for us to facilitate it.

Besides, from a first level existence point of view (the Greater Intelligence) this is not possible because it would require that the expanding energy, that forms the lead ball in question, would need to stop expanding and start contracting and this is a universe that needs to expand to support the intelligence of the Greater Intelligence and the universe exists with the sole purpose of supporting that intelligence as described in part three. So, once again, this is why I said that only in *theory* could the ball become so small as to pass back through the window.

So that addresses the fact that the ball is not anywhere near as small as it can get but that is not the end of it. It has to be said that the difference between the current size of the lead ball and that of its smallest extent (the single dimensional window) is the same as that between it and its largest extent (the size of the universe) which is even greater than the enormous original V_1 size from which the energy was reduced to form the ball in the first place. So, in a manner of speaking, it is always half way between the two limits of its size of which V_1 forms only a small fraction.

I'll try that one again. As I described in part three, the universe is such that a single dimensional energy window forms a seamless joint between the largest and smallest objects in the universe, i.e. the universe itself and each and every fundamental particle within, with the centre passing through all. This is rather like being on the circumference of a circle. If you consider a point on the opposite side of the circumference that always remains directly opposite you, it would be half way round in either direction. This would continue to be the case no matter where you choose to stand on the circumference. The seamless joint that forms the beginning and the end could not be realised because it *is* seamless. This is also the case with the energy window, and therefore unavailable as a datum. No matter how big you might think you are in the universe, you are always half way between your largest and smallest extent of your size unless you could pin point the location of the energy window to use as a datum and I'm afraid our human senses are not capable of that even when passing through it. (Sounds bizarre? You bet! Outside of convention, reality often is).

To return to our lead ball: even a sizeable further reduction in volume, as could be accommodated by our limited human means, would make not the slightest measurable difference in the gravitational effects that the lead ball would exhibit or, indeed to its measurable mass. (Mass is measured by use of inertia and the subtle aspects that need to be appreciated in this respect are addressed in the next book).

So at our level of observation, it would seem that no matter how we might condense matter it still seems to have the same mass.

To recap on the aspect of introducing expansion into the universe: if it were expanding, the ratio (as we shall see later) becomes not a ratio of change in volume but a ratio of one rate of expansion compared to another, producing exactly the same effect but this time (with the expanding universe) being the true state of affairs - "true" as in second level existence "true." More of that later.

Conclusion

So where does all this leave our two condensed spheres in the sponge model (which is not expanding), with respect to Newton's $m \times m/d^2$? How does this relationship apply? We can certainly see that the mass of each sphere is represented by the ratio V_1/V_2 which represents the degree to which each has condensed. We also know that the greater this ratio is, the more they attract each other, so the 'm×m' proportion holds true.

Similarly, we know from the sponge model with just one condensed sphere in it, that the tug, or gravity, emanates out from the surface of each sphere in such a way as to diminish by the square of the distance from their centres. Therefore the further each moves from the other the smaller becomes the gravitational attraction that each exerts on the other. Becoming smaller by the square of their distance apart. And conversely, as they move toward each other their gravitational attraction increases proportionately. The inverse square law also holds true. The net result being that Newton's law of universal gravitation - $m \times m/d^2$ - holds true in this model.

Now, I'm not saying that the universe is a sponge, only that it is a closed system of energy that we can talk about by referring to it as a sponge. Also, I am not saying that a lump of matter like that of a lead ball, is composed of one volume of energy condensed down to a smaller volume. What I am presenting is a static model in which the lead ball is composed of smaller particles which in turn appear to be composed of energy that has condensed into a smaller volume. I say "appear" because the true state of affairs is that each particle is not composed of condensed energy but energy which is not expanding at the same rate as its surroundings. The two have the same result but the first is simpler to understand at this stage. We shall look at expansion, in its full glory, later.

It doesn't matter where these discrete volumes of energy come from to form the likes of the lead ball. As far as the rest of the universe is concerned, the lead ball appears to have formed from a single large volume of energy, that has gathered in from its surroundings, condensing down to that of the ball, or any other lump of matter, and consequently behaves as such in terms of its gravitational field. It is just as easy to refer to it as being formed from a single volume of energy for the purpose of explanation.

Bubble model

So far I have placed the principle of mass and distance into context with respect to the effect of gravity produced by the formation of matter in a closed system with no gaps in it. Or more precisely; the effect of gravity which is produced when matter is formed by the act of the substance of that system (energy) condensing into a smaller volume. But the sponge model, used to demonstrate this effect, is a non fluid system so all we can see is tendencies. The two condensed spheres (representative of two masses) tend (want to) draw towards each other. But they are stopped from moving to the point of making surface to surface contact because they are locked in a non-fluid system that halts their movement when all the various tugs within the sponge balance out. This is a constraint because the universe does not behave like this in the presence of matter, moreover, the universe behaves as though it is a fluid system.

To see what I mean by "fluid," I offer the following bubble model. Next time you are having a bubble bath, observe two lonely bobbles that are situated far enough from any other bubbles so as not to effect them. If you sit still long enough the two lonely bubbles will eventually pull themselves together until they touch, accelerating as they get closer. If we considered the bubbles as being representative of mass and the 'tug' between them as representing gravity, we can see that these 'masses' are free to move to the point that they meet. Their movement, on the two dimensional surface of the water, is fluid.

If we could somehow pull them back apart without bursting them, they would again move back to each other when we let go. Move them far enough apart and they will fall under the influence of other bubbles or a nearby edge. Bring them close again but from a different angle of approach and again they move to each other. Introduce another bubble in close proximity and all three move together. If the third bubble was much bigger than the two original bubbles, they are keener to move toward *it* as opposed to each other.

We can play whatever tune we like within the confines of the two dimensions of the surface of the water and an effect of attraction can be observed as governed by the size and location of all the participating bubbles with respect to one another. This describes two dimensional fluidity in that the full extent of two dimensional movement, available on the surface of the water, is fully utilised under the influence of the constituent members that form that surface. This is contrary to the three dimensional sponge model whereby the constituent members are locked within it, only able to portray tendencies of movement and not movement to a full extent.

The attraction between bubbles on the surface of water can be loosely seen as a two dimensional representation of the sponge model because there is a tug set up by each bubble that emanates through the surface layer of the water molecules which diminishes outwards in direct proportion to the distance from each bubble. Not the square of the distance because we are talking about a two dimensional effect, not three.

To make clear: drop a pebble into a still pond and ripples radiate out. The circumference of any one ripple is seen to become greater in direct proportion to its radius from the centre. Whatever the circumference might be of a ripple at one distance from the centre, it is sure to be twice that circumference at twice that distance from the centre. The amount of energy that went into the first position of the ripple is the same amount as has gone into the second position but has had to spread itself twice as thinly. The ripple therefore diminishes as it radiates out from the source in direct proportion to the distance.

So, the attraction that each bubble places on the other is diminished as their distance apart increases. Conversely, if their distance becomes less then the attraction becomes greater, which is why they can be seen to accelerate as they draw near. This is an attraction facilitated by not only the tug that each bubble emanates throughout the surface but equally the tug that the rest of the surface places on each bubble as a result of the surface "doing something about" being robbed of the molecules that went into forming the bubbles. It can be said that the surface pulled the bubbles together just as the bubbles pulled themselves together.

By looking down onto the top of any one bubble, we can see how it is that the rest of the surface feels that the bubble has robbed the surface of molecules. The bubble is bowed upwards by the air coming to the surface and in so doing, the number of molecules that now occupies the surface area through which that air sliced on its journey up through the surface, has increased. Remembering that we are considering just the top two dimensional surface area of the water and not three dimensions such that we would then have to include height from the surface. From the point of view of the strictly two dimensional world of the surface of the water, an increase in height of the bubble molecules would not be obvious. It would think that the molecules had gathered into a smaller area and thereby constitute an increase in density against which the surface would tug. You can see how this approximately resembles the sponge model, with an increase in density of the red spheres result-ing in a tug emanating throughout the blue sponge.

Tank model

So let's go the whole hog and see if we can't create a three (four, to give density) dimensional fluid model by way of a flexible tank, full to the brim with water. Let's also seal it with a lid such that no air is left inside. This time, with the clamp of our imagination, let's cause two spherical volumes to condense and see what happens. I am of course making use of the tiny compressibility of water, in fact (given that this is a thought experiment) let's give our water heaps of compressibility to exaggerate the effects.

Sadly, once the two spherical regions have condensed they do not behave like the sponge model. They are not the least bit interested in wanting to exhibit three dimensional fluid movement toward each other for the very reason that it *is* a three dimensionally fluid system.

If this was a non-fluid system like the sponge model, once the regions had condensed, the material between the regions would have increased in density under the influ-ence of the force emanating from the surface of each con-densed region which would then result in a "sustained attraction" between them. By which I mean; two condensed red spheres in the sponge model would increase the density of sponge between them by the act of condensing. If the sponge between them has increased in density, then the two condensed regions cannot help but move toward each other under, what could be interpreted as, the influence of an at-traction. The attraction will remain for as long as the re-gions remain condensed. Therefore, for as long as the regions *do* remain condensed, there will be a *sustained at-traction*. The amount by which the intervening material would condense would be dependant upon the distance apart (due to the $1/d^2$ relationship) and the amount by which the regions have condensed. But, because the tank model is a fluid system, the molecules of water are at liberty to move however they wish, resulting in an unchanged density throughout that would provide no sustained attraction between the condensed regions.

The reason for this lies in the essence of the difference between the non-fluidity of the sponge and the fluidity of the water. The particles of sponge are fixed such that they always remain in the same position relative to their neighbours, even though the material is able to stretch, compress and generally deform. This attribute gives rise to a sustained increase in density between the condensed spheres that constitutes a continuous attraction between them. In the case of the water, however, the particles (or molecules) are indifferent to wanting to stay-put relative to their neighbours (because they form a fluid). They therefore shuffle about to their hearts desire. The result is an unchanged uniform density throughout the water considered separately of the condensed regions once those regions have condensed. If the density is unchanged then there can be no increase in density between the regions that would otherwise pull them together. The condensed regions can move freely without being the least bit interested in each other by way of an attraction. This free movement can otherwise be described as *fluid* movement and it is a fluid attraction (free to move from any angle to the point of touching) between the condensed regions that I am after so as to mimic the behaviour of gravity: like the two dimensional fluid behaviour of bubbles on the surface of water. So how can I hope to achieve it?

If we could prevent this aspect of fluidity (that allows the molecules to slip past each other) by insisting that they behave like the non-fluid sponge and remain in the same position relative to each other, we would see an effect that modelled gravity that would allow the two condensed regions to behave as we normally see gravity behave. That is, by pulling them together in order to make face to face contact. Given that this is a thought experiment, in which we are limited only by the power of our imagination, let's do just that:-

Once condensed, the regions would have drawn closer together by the effect of an increase in density between them which is *not* offset by the molecules being able to shuffle about. The distance between them would now be smaller. Knowing the inverse-square-law of the force coming from the surface of the condensed regions is such that the force increases as the distance becomes smaller, the force between them would then be greater because they are closer together. So the intervening material would again want to increase in density as affected by that increased force. As a result, they would again move that bit closer and again, the force between them would go up. And so on until they met face to face, accelerating as they went because the force would be gradually increasing between them as the distance becomes smaller (much as the bubbles accelerate as they draw closer). But as they ploughed closer together, we would need to have returned some of the fluid aspect that we had previously removed from the force-transmitting-molecules that lie between the condensed regions (transmitting the force by increasing in density). But only to the extent of allowing them to be gradually displaced sideways by the movement of the condensed regions coming together - "getting out of the way," in other words. The result is three dimensional fluid movement of the condensed regions that was facilitated by making the system non-fluid in certain aspects. Cheating, in other words.

The reason the bubble model was not subject to the same constraint was that although the bubbles were free to move two dimensionally on the surface, the tug transmitting molecules that formed the rest of the surface, were encouraged to stay put by the molecules underneath. In other words, we had a two dimensional *fluid* system on the surface, but which was *non*-fluid in the third dimension of up and down. This served to keep the surface molecules in place so as to transmit the varying degree of tug from the edge of one bubble to another. These tug transmitting molecules were then displaced as the bubbles drew together under the influence of that tug.

So where does this leave us. All this effort to work up to a model that shows how a three dimensional (four, including density) system, which is closed and has no gaps in it, models gravity when two regions within it are condensed, just to find it doesn't! Unless I cheat. One hell of a constraint considering I'm suggesting the universe is a four dimensional, closed, *apparently fluid* system with no gaps in it!

Well, yet again, a constraint points the way forward. There is one aspect missing and that is expansion and this is the aspect that causes this constraint of fluidity to disappear on the way to reality (second level existence "reality," in the form of the ultimate model that we call the expanding universe). If there was not such a constraint, I would, at this juncture, not be presenting a model. It would be reality itself in the form of the ultimate model and expansion would not be needed. At the moment we are not looking at an expanding model, we are looking at a static model in which I will now put all the ground work hither to covered into the ultimate model, minus expansion, and totally ignore this constraint. I can ignore it because I know I can solve it by showing how the universe is *apparently* fluid. That is, by being fluid in some respects and non-fluid in others, and without the need for any cheating! More on this in part five.

CHAPTER 5
THE NON-EXPANDING ULTIMATE
MODEL

Overview

So what have we so far? We know from part three that the universe is constructed from energy that is continually expanding out into four dimensions in the form of a four dimensional roll. But that was a universe that was in the act of continuously expanding and we are presently looking at a universe that has expanded and stopped - for the sake of explanation. That was also a system that had no matter in it - just a soup of smooth expanding energy. The sponge, bubble and tank models were all designed to see what happens when matter forms. So I must hope to perpetuate this in the form of now introducing matter into a system that is *still* not expanding so as to sustain simplicity of explanation. Such a system would then mimic the ultimate model of reality (which is the universe as we see and experience it) without the aspect of expansion. I can but call that system the non-expanding ultimate model: a model of a model, or submodel which could equally be regarded as a **"static model."**

To do this I need to scale things up so the matter I shall introduce would have to be an astronomical body like the Moon, Earth, Sun, a meteorite or whatever. I will ignore three dimensional movement (whizzing about) apart from the displacement caused under the influence of gravity. As you might suppose, this model is nothing more than the transposition of the previous models into a non-expanding universe but it will also serve to introduce the concept of the primary forces at work within the universe.

Gravity in the non-expanding ultimate model

So, purely from a non-expanding point of view, for the universe to reach a state of having been expanded it must first have undergone the act of expanding to get there. From part three, chapter three, subheading "Energy as the prime mover," it can be seen that it is the act of reducing energy that *then* causes an increase in volume because the universe is unbound (because it has no edge with which to prevent the expansion). So the universe expanded by the act of reducing energy levels at each and every location within it. The cause of this expansion will be detailed in part five but for now it would be a lot easier to simply regard it as a **"force of expansion"** and say that it has effectively served to stretch out energy into the four dimensions of density to form a static universe that we are currently examining.

If the force of expansion were to disappear, the single dimension of energy would contract back from its stretched four dimensional state and return to a single dimension with no additional three dimensional extension. A sort of universal collapse being prevented by the force of expansion.

From the previous models we can see how matter is formed by the act of a certain quantity of this energy condensing into a smaller three dimensional location as compared to that which it previously occupied (V_1/V_2). Like that, an astronomical body would have to be formed by the coming together of many smaller particles of matter, each formed by its own V_1/V_2 process. Once gathered, they can be equally viewed as an astronomical object having formed from one giant V_1/V_2 process. It makes little difference how you view it from a macroscopic point of view because we

Part 4: Gravity, Matter and Mass

are about to consider astronomical bodies as being the principle particles of matter. By which I mean that we are currently looking at the large scale universe and how gravity comes about within it. So we need not bother delving any deeper than the principle lumps of matter that generate that gravitational effect. That will come in book three which forms part of this same theory. By looking only at the principle lumps of matter as being formed from one giant V_1/V_2 process the explanation becomes simpler and therefore one that I am going to stick with. Besides, this is exactly how the universe 'feels' that these large lumps of matter have been formed.

If the body in question has effectively formed by a giant V_1/V_2 process, then the energy that has gone into forming it is energy that the universe as a whole will see as being robbed from its constituency just as the overall sponge felt that the condensed red sphere had nicked some of its material and wanted to do something about it by way of trying to tug it back. This "doing something about it" is a situation that also manifests itself within this "non-expanding ultimate model." The force of expansion is trying to maintain the entire universe at a uniform level of expansion throughout. This would then provide a uniform density of energy throughout. By then having part of its constituency condense into a region of high density of energy means that the **force of expansion** has no choice but to tug on the region so as to try and expand it back out to its original density. The amount by which it tugs is equal to the amount of energy gone into forming that lump of matter. Likewise, the matter tugs back against the force of expansion in an effort to maintain its newly formed mass. The force that caused the matter to form is detailed later.

The tug that is set up throughout the system, obviously emanates from the surface of the matter and diminishes by the inverse square of the distance from the centre of that

131

matter as per the sponge model. We are therefore looking at the gravitational field that the astronomical body generates.

It now becomes obvious that it is all a question of forces: the force that causes energy to condense into matter, and the force that is trying to maintain a uniform level of expansion throughout the system. The resulting tug set up between the two is what we see as gravity. A tug that diminishes by the inverse square of the distance simply because it is being transmitted through a three dimensional system (four to include density).

Cause a second body of matter to form in just the same way as the first and the two will attract each other in the same fashion as the two condensed spheres in the sponge model ($m \times m / d^2$). In fact they will actually move towards each other to the point of making contact if we cheat as we did in the tank model and call this a fluid system that behaves like a non-fluid in certain respects.

As always, this reality can be viewed from a different angle and be explained as follows: both bodies are fighting a finely balanced battle by resisting the will of the universe in its bid to expand them both back out and regain its lost energy. This battle is especially in evidence between the two bodies where the universe is trying to expand both bodies simultaneously towards each other and, in the absence of anything to stop them, the universe draws them towards each other. Likewise, in their desperate bid to prevent this expansion (and maintain their mass) they are equally guilty of unwittingly drawing *themselves* together under the influence of gravity.

Universal forces

Once the first body had formed, the **force of expansion** tugged upon it as a result of its formation. When the second body formed the **force of expansion** then had an additional amount of tugging to do. As we shall see later, the force that causes the matter to form (presently what we can call "the clamp of our imagination"), once applied, is unyielding; it is constant in its application regardless of the deformation of the energy upon which it is forcing. Like the sponge model in which the overall shape reduced in size due to the formation of the condensed red sphere within, the universe also reduces in size as matter forms within. The size to which I refer is the three dimensional outer most extension. In the real expanding universe this extension is the point at which energy rolls off having past through zero density which is the location of the single dimensional energy window. Chapter three, subheading "Closed system" in part three, further explains how this reduction in the universe's three dimensional size comes about.

The net result of the formation of matter in such a system is to produce a balance of forces which amounts to nothing more than a tug between two different sources. One source is the force of expansion and the other is the force used to cause a body of matter to form (in this case, the clamp of our imagination). To see this more clearly we can return to our sponge model with just one condensed red sphere in it. The deformation of the blue sponge is as a result of the red sphere condensing and the blue sponge tugs back as a consequence of "doing something about it." This "tugging back" is equivalent to the "force of expansion." The force that caused the red sphere to condense is due to the clamp of our imagination. The clamp of our imagination produces a force which in turn results in a condensing of sponge to give us the red condensed sphere but the size to which that region of sponge condenses is a function of the difference between the force of the blue sponge pulling back and the force employed by the clamp of our imagination. If, for some reason, the force of the blue sponge pulling back were to increase, the size to which the condensed region has reduced also increases regardless of the fact that the force produced by the clamp of our imagination has remained constant.

So, what might cause the blue sponge to increase its "pulling back" effect? Well, if we caused a second region of sponge to condense under the force of a second clamp of our imagination, the blue sponge could not help but tug back all the more. In doing so it would tug that much more on the first condensed sphere and cause it to expand slightly.

To see how this works in the ultimate non-expanding model we can say that by the formation of the second body (facilitated once again by the clamp of our imagination - the true cause of which will be identified later) the poor old force of expansion now has an additional force pulling in opposition to it. But by whatever degree the additional "clamp of imagination" force pulls against the force of expansion, is exactly the same additional degree by which the force of expansion will pull back. The existing "clamp of imagination" force (that which caused the first body of matter to form) is still pulling against the same force of expansion and therefore sees it pulling back that much more as a result of the second body of matter forming. If the force of expansion has increased by virtue of the second formation of matter, and the force that caused the first body to form is unchanging, then the first body of matter will start to lose its finely balanced tug of war against the force of expansion and expand slightly as a result. It will expand until the two forces again balance out. Like this we can see that the first piece of matter 'feels' the presence of the other, regardless of where they are situated with respect to each other within the same system, as reflected in their level of expansion (or density of energy, or volumetric size - all the same).

This, once again, demonstrates how this is a closed system because the effect of a disturbance is transmitted (or 'felt') throughout the whole. When a second lump of matter forms in the universe, the first lump of matter would expand as a result. And what's more, if a third forms, the first two expand as a result, and so on. They are each indirectly 'feeling' the existence of the others no matter where they are situated with respect to one another within the universe.

CHAPTER 6
GRAVITY IN AN EXPANDING
UNIVERSE

Overview

At this juncture the concept of a universe which is expanding will now be introduced to fall fully in line with the model described in part three. The model described in the last chapter is a static model for the sake of explanation. It will be 'rerun' in this chapter, in a dynamic form; in terms of an expanding universe. This chapter will show how, if an area of expanding energy has a slower rate of expansion relative to the rate of expansion of the surrounding energy (space) then matter is created which exhibits the phenomena of gravity in precisely the same manner as described in the foregoing chapters; because it will appear to have condensed.

As stated at the end of the section under the subheading "Tank model" in this part of the book, the aspect of expansion now overcomes the constraint of the universe being composed of what appears to be fluid energy because expansion causes energy to behave like a non-fluid when we look at gravity. But, as I said there, I will address this in part five. Until then I ask that we ignore the constraint because the answer gives us a system that behaves just as I am about to explain.

In this chapter the aspect of expansion will be seen to overcome another constraint that makes itself apparent in the static model. That is; if something condenses such as the spheres in the sponge model or the matter in the non-expanding model, then you would expect there to be some kind of gap that becomes smaller in order to facilitate the condensing of energy into a smaller volume. This is contrary to the fact that I have said that the universe is a system which has no gaps in it. However, in the expanding model, nothing actually condenses and therefore nothing needs to be compressed. It only appears to be compressed relative to its surroundings because its surroundings are expanding faster than it.

This chapter will make obvious the fact that it is not just space which is expanding (as is currently believed) in this four dimensionally expanding shape (universe), but everything in it as well, i.e. including the matter contained within. It will go further to state that a universe (including the matter within) which is not continually expanding is one in which matter, and therefore gravity, could not manifest itself because gravity and matter are as a result of different rates of expansion. A universe in which only space (low level, and therefore apparently massless energy) is expanding, would not be capable of constructing anything. Gravity would not work in the second level of existence, and thereby not enable the Greater Intelligence to 'think', from its own first level existence point of view.

Review

So, what does all that mean? In chapter three "The Non-Expanding Universe," in this part of the book, I explained how we can remove the aspect of expansion in an otherwise continuously expanding universe by seeing things as they appear to us. Namely, that matter is not expanding. From this simplistic point of view we were able to go on to explore how matter, if condensed (or contracted), exhibits the phenomena of gravity when formed *from* and being *in* a closed system with no gaps in it. More precisely, we were able to see the effects of a force that radiates out from the surface of the condensed material that is called a gravitational field. And further, how that gravitational field interacts with other fields to produce an attraction between bodies of matter which is proportional to Newton's law of universal gravitation: $m \times m/d^2$.

If we are now to see matter as expanding along with the space between matter, I must hope to transpose those same gravitational effects across from the static model to this expanding (and therefore a dynamic model) and keep them intact. This is exactly what I am about to do.

Transposition from static to dynamic

The matter that was previously described as forming by the act of gathering energy into a smaller volume in accordance with the V_1/V_2 ratio, has the equivalent, in the real second level existence *expanding* universe, of being energy which is not expanding at the same rate as its neighbouring faster expanding energy. So V_1/V_2 **becomes the ratio of "original rate of expansion of V_1 at the time of formation" over "reduced rate of expansion."** Under the earlier heading of "Mass" I used V_1/V_2 to describe the mass of a body which has undergone the reduction in size from V_1 to V_2, so the dynamic equivalent of that is also "original rate of expansion of V_1 at the time of formation" over "reduced rate of expansion."

To see things more clearly let's look at our lead ball, as mentioned before, and view it as having formed from a very large volume of energy condensed down to a smaller volume (V_1/V_2) as opposed to being formed from many smaller lumps of matter each complete with its own V_1/V_2 ratio (the result, from the macroscopic point of view, is the same). Let's also imagine that this lead ball is the only piece of matter that is about to form in a universe void of any other matter with a uniform low level of energy throughout.

Part 4: Gravity, Matter and Mass

Before V_1 decided to condense, it had the same density of energy as its surroundings. Just like the spherical volume of sponge that we painted red before it condensed to a smaller volume in the sponge model - before it condensed it had the same density as the blue coloured material that formed the rest of the sponge. The dynamic equivalent of that model (before the sphere condensed) would be that the red and blue coloured sponge is continuously expanding at the same rate to provide the same density of sponge throughout[1]. Likewise, V_1 condensing down to form the lead ball, has the dynamic equivalence of simply deciding not to expand at the same rate as the rest of the expanding energy (V_1 has not condensed at all). The rest of the expanding area does not know itself to be expanding. How can it? It has no reference against which to gauge the fact that it is expanding, apart from, that is, the V_1 volume which it now sees as getting smaller because V_1 is expanding at a slower rate than *it*.

The conversation amongst the constituent members that forms the rest of the energy, considered separately of the V_1 volume, would go something like this: "what do you reckon to that then! There's a spherical volume of energy over there that appears to have got smaller. It can't have lost any of its constituent energy because there is nowhere for it to go. So the same quantity of energy must have formed into a smaller volume and thereby become more dense. It seems to have contracted! I don't know how this is possible because we collectively form a system that is

---

[1]   *As described in part three, the closer you get to the edge of the universe, the faster it is expanding. Therefore, the density is not uniform throughout all of so called "empty space." The density would gradually reduce towards the edge. But given the enormous size of the universe, this change in density can be ignored for the purpose of localised formation of matter.*

139

closed with no gaps in it. And yet that spherical volume must have compressed some kind of gap within itself to produce the effect of contraction."

In fact, the conversation amongst the surface molecules in the bubble model would be very similar. They would conclude amongst themselves that an area, which we know to be the location of a bubble, had somehow gathered water molecules together to present itself as an area of increased density. This is because they are unaware of the third dimension of up/down. They would not know that the molecules had increased in number within a certain area because they had simply bulged upwards to form the bubble. They are not in possession of all the facts just as we would not be if we were looking directly down on top of the water and didn't appreciate that the molecules were bulging up towards us.

This "not being in possession of all the facts" is the case for the expanding energy that surrounds the V_1 volume. What the energy does not realise is that the V_1 volume and itself are expanding, with V_1 expanding at a slower rate. No gaps are necessary to afford any kind of compression. The "getting smaller" that the surrounding energy witnesses is the equivalent, within the static model, of V_1 *condensing*. That is not to say that V_1 appears to go on condensing infinitum. It 'condenses' to whatever the difference is between the rate of expansion of the surrounding energy compared to that of the slower expanding V_1, and there it stops. Remaining at a steady comparative density. The relative size at which it stops condensing is the static equivalent to V_2. So the dynamic (real world) ratio is not V_1/V_2 in order to represent its degree of condensing energy or mass, but the ratio of one rate-of-expansion over the other.

Once the sphere has finished forming, it manifests itself as a lump of matter. When enough of these lumps have come together in the same locality we might call it a lead ball. Put into real world terms: we do not look at a lead ball and say "struth! look at this ball, see how it is not expanding as fast as its surroundings thereby appearing to be energy which is concentrated into an extent that is equal to its mass times the square of the speed of light" ($E = mc^2$). No. We would be more inclined to say "look at this ball which has energy which has condensed down into a smaller volume to present itself as being equivalent to its mass times the square of the speed of light." We don't realise that we and our surroundings are expanding and therefore blame the ball for condensing when really it is simply not expanding as fast as its surroundings. Things are not what they appear!

Returning to the lead ball as being the only piece of matter in the universe: the rest of the energy, apart from that forming the matter in question, would have a gravitational field emanating through it, from the surface of the ball, for the same reason as described in the sponge model and the non-expanding ultimate model.

To see what I mean by the equivalence between the sponge (static) model and the expanding version, the view one should adopt is that of the expanding energy surrounding the lead ball. As the region of retarded-rate-of-expansion (the lead ball) is expanding, along with the surrounding area, part of which you form, your eye would also be expanding and therefore the whole set-up *appears* to you as being static (not expanding). The retarded region appears to have condensed. This way we can still say that the surrounding region can be viewed as being made up of spherical shells, just as we argued that the blue sponge surrounding the condensed red sphere in the sponge model could be regarded as shells of gradually increasing size. This means we haven't got to worry about the rather complicated issue of the surrounding shells, and lead ball, being in a state of continuous expansion. All we need to do is *bear in mind* that the shells are expanding, we haven't got to try to see them actually doing it. This then enables us to get an idea of what is going on in this expanding system without the complication of expansion, except now we cannot be talking of "tug" in quite the same way as we did in the sponge model. The expanding equivalent would be as follows:-

The wall of the ball would not form a stepped interface between the two rates of expansion (going straight from one rate of expansion to the other at the location of the wall). The rate of expansion would slowly increase towards that of far-out surrounding space as we observe larger and larger shells from the wall of the ball. Or equally, as *measured* from the centre of the ball. Until it reaches the same rate of expansion as the rest of the far-out space/universe.

The rate at which it increases in rate-of-expansion is proportional to the square of the distance from the centre of the ball. Or, I could equally say that the rate at which the rate-of-expansion *reduces* is proportional to the ***inverse square of the distance***. Both statements give the same result but in the second version of the same statement the terms *"reduces"* and *"inverse"* cancel each other out to give, once again, an increasing rate of expansion with respect to the square of the distance. The reason I bother with such play on words is because it shows that the inverse square law still holds true even in this expanding model.

It can't be otherwise. This is another manifestation of the inverse square law because we are talking about different rates of expansion on shells of increasing three dimensional size as we observe further out from the centre. The effect of the ball expanding at a slower rate places a force on the rest of the surrounding universe. This is a force that radiates out in three dimensions and that remains constant, having the effect of slowing down the rate of expansion of the medium through which it travels. This is a medium which becomes larger as the force travels through it (by "becomes larger" I mean the gradually increasing size of shells that we don't need to try and visualise as actually expanding as I explained earlier). If the force is remaining constant but making its presence felt through ever increasing size of shells, then the same amount of force is having to spread itself more thinly as it goes. Geometry tells us that the size of the shells, through which the force is acting, will increase by the square of the distance. So the force, taken along a radial line drawn from the surface of the ball (inline with the centre), will see a "slowing-down force" which will diminish by the inverse square of the distance from the centre of the ball.

The net result is that as the force spreads itself more thinly at a rate equal to the inverse of the square of the distance from the centre, the slowing effect that the force has on the expanding energy through which it travels, must diminish by the same rate as measured along the radial line. The energy would expand at the rate that it previously expanded (before the ball formed by the act of a quantity of energy having a retarded rate of expansion) minus an amount proportional to the inverse square of the distance along the radial line. In other words, the *change in* rate of expansion (<u>compared to that which prevailed before the ball formed into matter</u>), is proportional to the inverse square of the distance as measured from the centre, along the radial line - a gravitational field. It is important to remember the qualification (underlined) of what is meant by "change in" (see also figure two on page 150).

But just a minute! Surely expansion and density are the same thing. If a given region has a low rate of expansion, it must be more dense than a region with a high rate of expansion and we now know that the *change in* rate of expansion, as we observe out on a radial line from the surface of the ball (matter), follows the inverse square law as measured from the centre. This means there must be a *change in* density gradient along this line that follows the same law. So we can now say that for "change in density of energy" we can read "intensity of gravitational field." Change in density of energy, and gravitational field being one and the same phenomena. This is what I would interpret as being what is conventionally called "the warping of space" with space and energy being the same thing. And, just like the static model, this gravitational field interacts with that produced by the formation of other particles of matter to provide a gravitational attraction which follows Newton's equation $m \times m/d^2$.

The gravitational effect on the mass of matter

So, as two bodies of matter draw closer together under the influence of gravity, they each experience increasing density of space/energy as a result of each others "warping of space" or gravitational field, that exists between themselves and the rest of the universe.

This means that as far as each body is concerned, as it draws closer to its neighbour, it travels further into energy of increasing density. This makes each advancing body of matter feel as if the force of expansion (the force produced by the universe in trying to expand matter at the same rate as itself) is easing off on its tug against the force that caused the bodies to form in the first place (formed by energy expanding at a slower rate - the clamp of our imagination, for the present). It appears to the immediate vicinity of energy around each body as though the universe is demanding less by way of returned energy (a lowering energy demand) of which it has been robbed during the fabrication of the matter within each body. This provides a reduction in energy demand that would otherwise 'pull' the advancing bodies out in the form of an increased rate of expansion in order to return all of the lost energy (of which the universe feels it has been robbed) which indeed it would if the bodies' mass retaining force (clamp of our imagination) were to allow it. If the universe's force of expansion has eased off, then the force (which is represented by the clamp of our imagination - which remains constant) now has the advantage and the body of matter expands at a slower rate. In static terms; its V_2 becomes smaller. Given that the original rate of expansion of V_1 always remains constant from the time of formation of the body of matter, the ratio of original rate of expansion over the reduced rate of expansion becomes greater, i.e. its mass must increase. It would increase in proportion to the **change in** density of energy that it experiences as it moves closer to its neighbour which is proportional to the inverse of the square of the distance.

Unification between Einstein and Newton

Earlier we looked at a lead ball that was suspended near another that was fixed and asked what would happen if our dangling friend was condensed and thereby increased in mass. The effect, we said, would be impossible to measure because the sort of compression we could afford was negligible, to say the least, compared to the enormous limits of its two extensions of size; big and small. This still holds true with regard to the effect of increased mass under the influence of gravity. But if we were able to offer up a very large lump of matter, say; the planet Mercury, as close as we can to an even bigger mass, say; the Sun, we might expect to see some noticeable change in mass.

Now, the discrepancy between Newton's law of gravity and that of Einstein's is such that Newton's law could do with a touch more mass to bring it in line with Einstein's when it comes to the precession of the perihelion of Mercury's orbit as it draws closest to the Sun. Just such an increase in mass would come as a result of their two gravitational fields on each other. With Newton's equation $m \times m / d^2$ a small increase in either or both of the 'm's (mass) gives a drop more gravity that is needed to produce the slowly precessing perihelion of Mercury. Quite apart, that is, from the additional mass that may or may not be afforded by the effect of velocity, which I will cover in the next book under the broad heading of movement within the universe.

But whose mass is increasing. The Sun's or Mercury's? Well, it would have to be both because both are subject to the same laws of an ordered universe (a cosmos). But the Sun has a V_1/V_2 (speaking in terms of the static model) far in excess of Mercury's and the tiny amount by which Mercury's gravity effects the Sun, in terms of increasing its mass, would be just that; tiny. The effect, on the other hand, of the Sun on Mercury would be greater because the V_1/V_2 of Mercury is that much smaller and a further reduction of V_2 would be more pronounced. Even though the effect would still be unbelievably small and becoming even smaller as we look at the orbits of the other planets further out from the Sun. This is why the difference between Newton's law of gravity and that of Einstein's are indistinguishable for the planets further out.

We can now ask the question; if we were on Mercury as it draws near to the Sun, would we be able to measure this increase in Mercury's mass? No would be the answer. Each and every piece of matter on Mercury would be subject to the same increase in mass. By taking our mass measuring equipment there, you might expect to pick up a piece of this matter and measure its increase (assuming we knew its mass while Mercury was at a more distant point from the Sun during its elliptical orbit). But, quite apart from the fact that the increase would be impossible to measure, in absolute terms, the kit that we might take with us would increase in mass along with us and our spaceship as we journey from Earth to Mercury, because we would be passing through energy of increasing density under the gravitational influence of Mercury and the Sun. Whatever we take to Mercury as our reference, having been calibrated on our planet, would correspondingly increase in mass to show no change in mass of the object being measured, once we get there.

Similarly, as you stood on any astronomical body that was becoming closer to another, you would not be able to measure any change in size of the on coming body as it passes through the gravitational effect of increasing density of energy. This is because both would change in size according to the ratio of V_1/V_2 of each compared to the other in respect to their distance apart. *It* would become smaller and you and your astronomical body (upon which you are standing) would also become smaller. One relative to the other would be the same size with all measuring equipment and reference tools distorting proportionately to give constant readings as you draw nearer and nearer. The only change you *would* notice is the usual illusion of the on coming body getting bigger, just as a bus appears to grow in size as it travels down the road towards you.

(There is also the question of light being distorted from one to the other but light is one of the topics of the next book).

To summarise; the astronomical bodies attract each other because they are in a closed system from which they have been formed within. Each increasing in density as they move closer together, in absolute terms that is. Relatively speaking, each does not notice any change in density with respect to the other because they both increase in density proportionately to the other. Conversely, they would both reduce in density (expand) if they moved further apart for the inverse of the above reasoning. They are undergoing four dimensional movement, as I will explain next. But the mechanics of this is intriguing, to say the least, because it leads to a universe that is *both* expanding and apparently steady state at the same time, as I will explain in part five.

Four dimensional movement

So, by the formation of any number of bodies of matter, in the way that I have described, we can see that each will 'feel' the presence of all the others - by feeling their mutual gravitational effect. These are gravitational fields that each body of matter produces and which directly or indirectly, influences the three dimensional movement of all the other bodies of matter, where ever they might be in relation to one another, at any given time, within a system of which they all form an integral part. This is because the gravity of any one lump of matter, no matter how diminished it becomes, will radiate throughout the entire universe and interact with other fields of gravity, giving us a universe which is awash with gravitational fields amongst which all the bodies of matter must swim.

So when any lump of matter moves, be it under the influence of gravity or not, it cannot help but be effected by this "wash of gravity" in terms of its volume/mass, as described above. This then means that its density is effected, and density is four dimensional. From this, an interesting conclusion can be drawn - that no three dimensional movement is possible within the universe without experiencing a varying degree of gravity from other bodies. Which means that three dimensional movement cannot, in truth, be separated from four dimensional movement.

Remembering that three dimensional movement is "whizzing about" through a combination of the three conventional dimensions. And four dimensional movement is the combination of all three dimensions to give expansion, or contraction. If something expands or contracts its density must change and density is four dimensions. This, again, underlines the fact that this is a four dimensional universe.

PART 5

THE MIND OF OUR CREATOR AND THE ROLLING PIN OF ACADEMIC CRUCIFIXION

Energy is intelligence/substance/life. Energy cannot be destroyed and therefore supports life after death. If intelligence is energy and energy is expanding to form a four dimensional universe, the different rates of expansion of which forms matter, then matter is the input of data with which to be intelligent. The four dimensional expansion of a universe void of matter is consciousness and the formation of matter by the differing rates of expansion is then the process of thinking. Human beings play a central role in this process. Figure two provides an overview that will be explained throughout this last part of the book.

149

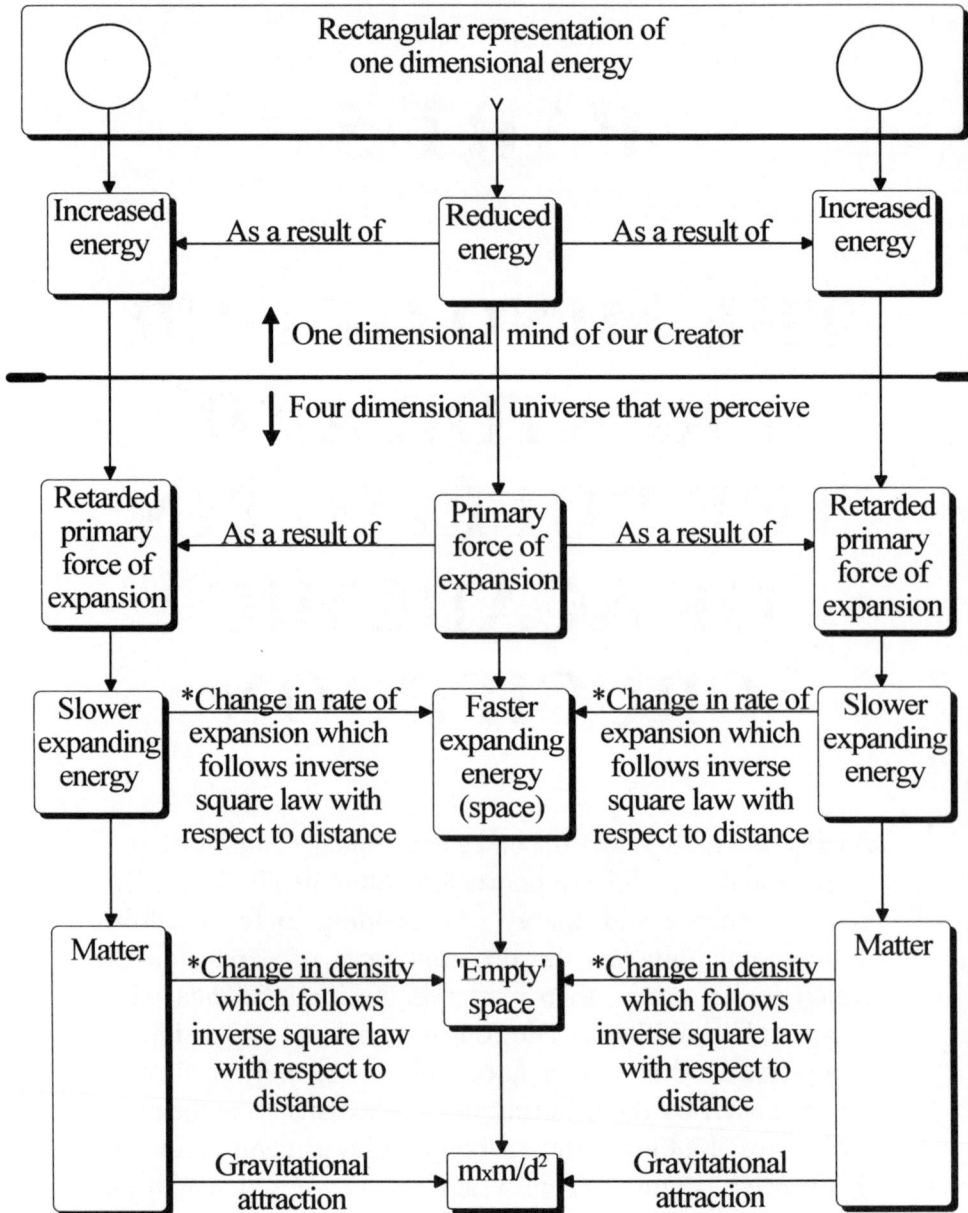

```
┌──────────────────────────────────────────────────────────────────┐
│  ◯         Rectangular representation of              ◯            │
│              one dimensional energy                               │
└──────────────────────────────────────────────────────────────────┘
```

Rectangular representation of one dimensional energy

Increased energy ←— As a result of —— Reduced energy —— As a result of —→ Increased energy

↑ One dimensional mind of our Creator

↓ Four dimensional universe that we perceive

Retarded primary force of expansion ←— As a result of —— Primary force of expansion —— As a result of —→ Retarded primary force of expansion

Slower expanding energy — *Change in rate of expansion which follows inverse square law with respect to distance → Faster expanding energy (space) ← *Change in rate of expansion which follows inverse square law with respect to distance — Slower expanding energy

Matter — *Change in density which follows inverse square law with respect to distance → 'Empty' space ← *Change in density which follows inverse square law with respect to distance — Matter

Gravitational attraction → $m \times m / d^2$ ← Gravitational attraction

* "change in:" compared to that which prevailed before the matter was formed
  - see the last two paragraphs on page 143 (extending onto page 144).

Figure 2

CHAPTER 1

THE MIND OF OUR CREATOR

We have seen the mechanics of the effects of various rates of expansion in the form of gravity and the formation of matter in part four, but what caused the energy to expand at these different rates in the first place?

If we follow the conventional route to answering this sort of question, we would look only at that which we experience to try and find the answer. By which I mean we would look within the universe *as we see it*, or rather; *as we conventionally understand it*, for a cause that provides the effect, but that is much like trying to lift yourself up by your own boot laces. It smacks of something like perpetual motion. Something from nothing. Matter is energy and as such energy is the 'substance' of all creation, to then look for that same energy, as we see it, to cause the effect of its own existence in the form of matter, would be like hoisting on those proverbial boot laces. It is quite simply impossible! It would be the act of frustrated human beings which lack the insight to the obvious.

The obvious is that the universe is pure intelligence, which is energy, which is the Greater Intelligence, or Creator, or whatever name you care to give it, him or her. It is the act of intelligence (thinking, although not thinking as we do) that causes energy to behave as it does. Not energy as a benign (not forming an intelligence) physical phenomena that somehow causes *itself* to behave as it does.

This would be like expecting a bicycle to turn itself into roof guttering all by itself: it won't unless we melt it down and reforge the material into that of the guttering. Even though it is the same material in both cases, it will not perform as we would hope without intellectual

151

intervention. In the case of the Greater Intelligence causing energy to behave as it does, it provides its own intrinsic intellectual intervention by being just that; pure intelligence. Bearing in mind that "intrinsic" means an inherent characteristic; something which unavoidably *is* by virtue of itself. For instance, if you are a fish you are *intrinsically* safe from drowning. In terms of the foregoing context: the Greater Intelligence is intelligence which is energy (one and the same) and given that all of creation is formed from energy, anything that happens within that creation must be as an intrinsic result of intelligence, not the intrinsic result of energy as a benign 'substance'.

Energy is not a substance?

It could now be argued that energy is not a substance, it is intelligence. Happiness is not a substance, the act of human thought is not a substance. It might appear to be supported by a "substance" in the form our brain cells but that is because we are part of the Greater Intelligence as discrete intelligences and as such our job is to see things as being a substance. This is by virtue of the four dimensions that intelligence affords us within our role of processing data: it is all in the mind!

But this statement should invoke an interesting response. In part one I argued that the physical universe can certainly be *called* physical because that is what we call it. But ultimately, the word physical has no meaning because there is no latitude of experience for it. We don't really know what is *not* physical in order to make a comparison and put "*is* physical" into context. I have also argued that all of existence is pure intelligence and that intelligence is supported by energy, therefore energy is intelligence. And what is more, I have said that there is a latitude of experience for intelligence so it can't be a meaningless word. If energy is intelligence and intelligence is all of existence, then energy can be regarded as a substance but only in the same way that all of existence (the universe) can be regarded as physical, because energy is intelligence which then has a latitude of experience so energy can be regarded as a substance but only by association with intelligence. By itself, energy could not be called a substance.

Let me put it another way. If we were to agree that our dreams are not physical and we all fell asleep for the rest of our days but were able to communicate with each other, who could honestly say that what they were experiencing is not physical or that what they touched was not a substance? If then our bodies were to die but somehow we kept on dreaming, then all that exists for us is our dream world, and again, could we say that it was not physical and not fall of objects of substance. We might have children in those dreams. How could we tell them that they are not physical and that the new motor bike for which they crave, is not a substance! The fact is that the universe, dream or not, IS WHAT IT IS and if people say it is energy in the form of substance, then that is what it is, but only because we think it is, and therefore by association with thought (intelligence).

"Dream-world" aside, this is an intelligence of which we form part in its likeness i.e. data processing sub-units that collectively help to form *it*. This is first level existence. Our job is to process data by experiencing and influencing what we call the universe with the existence of a "universe" being how we perceive things. This is second level existence (see figure one on page 12). The matter within that universe is the input of data by the Greater intelligence: that which it is considering. That's not to suggest that the Greater Intelligence thinks by popping matter in and out of second level existence. To a certain extent it must do this but more over, it is the unthinkable number of different manifestations and interactions of that matter, from the microscopic to the macroscopic and all it includes, that then provides for the processing of that data throughout all of creation (the universe) - which is the first level existence basis of rule three of the three simple rules detailed on pages 46 and 69.

Life after death

This grand scale processing of data is a process in which we take an active part. It is also a process that logically dictates that the Greater Intelligence is not a single intelligence, it is many interacting intelligences that provide for one overall entity as broadly described in chapter four, "The Meaning of Life" in part one. And finally, it is also a process that cannot help but support what we call life after death.

Turn your radio off - does the DJ die? I think not. He is still there when you turn it back on. Similarly, when, what we call "our physical manifestation," shuttles off the end of its mortal coil, the mind, which is the intelligence driving that physical being (and by virtue of which that physical being is able to manifest itself, as explained in part one) remains as part of the Greater intelligence. It is a data processing sub-unit that forms part of the Greater Intelligence and as a discrete element of intelligence it must be formed from just that: intelligence, which is energy.

As we know, energy cannot be destroyed or created, only relocated and that is precisely what happens. The 'dead' mind in question has completed its data processing activities in the form of its existence in the second level existence four dimensional universe and the four dimensions that such an existence afforded have now been withdrawn by the simple act of completing those activities. But as an intelligence (which is energy) its services will never be complete; it has more of the same duties to perform. From the point of view of those left behind and, when in possession of the knowledge of first level existence, we

154

would have to say it has gone to another place (another place by whatever name we might care to use).

Indeed, in effect it has gone to another dimension, the dimension of pure energy/intelligence which is a single dimension that forms first level existence. In fact it hasn't *gone* anywhere. It is exactly where it was in the first place: part of the Greater Intelligence. The processing of data is something we do under the guidance of free will (see part one) and, as I will explain in book four, that is governed by certain criteria that leads to the world in which we live. Once outside of this criteria, our intelligence experiences activities not based on lump, bump and thump, but on a higher level of intellectual processing and one, from our second level existence point of view, that is considerably more satisfying than our own.

If you think this has little to do with gravity, matter and mass, you are wrong. This is an holistic theory and as such anything and everything is one and the same. I could easily switch to toilet pans, quantum physics or love and suffering and still be totally in context by encompassing an ultimate explanation for all of creation. Creation handed down by the Greater Intelligence: our Creator (intrinsically handed down).

As you would therefore expect, there is much to be said on the concept of a Greater Intelligence alone, and I intend to say it in the form of the other books but for now we are looking at the simple "base case" and as such we need to look at the general mechanics of its mind. In particular, the cause of different rates of expansion as they manifest themselves to us within the only form of existence that we are capable of perceiving - for it is that form of existence for which we have been intrinsically designed; in the form that we know ourselves: for the second level existence universe.

The primary cause of expansion

There is only one cause of expansion (just as there is only one everything). This cause is that which gives rise to the expanding four dimensionally rolling universe of energy with no matter in it, as described in part three. But, as we have seen, this expansion is retarded within certain regions to then form matter. So I can say that effectively there are two rates of expansion having two causes. The first is caused by what I shall call the **primary force of expansion** (the rolling universe) and the second by what I shall call the **retarded primary force of expansion** (matter). They are both the same force of expansion but one is retarded when compared to the other. The varying degrees of retardation causes the varying attributes of matter as we see it.

One way to envisage this *force* is as I described before; as the 'clamp of our imagination'. Within the *expanding* universe it is not condensing anything, it is a force applied by the Greater intelligence that retards the rate of expansion to varying degrees which has the effect of *appearing* to have condensed. This force provides the input of data (the formation of matter) into the thinking mechanism (the universe). The universe then has its natural way by influencing the volume, mass and gravitational effects of that matter (input of data) in accordance with the environment in which that matter finds itself within the thinking mechanism that we call the universe. This matter then goes on to form every manifestation of matter in line with what we call "physical laws". The force that causes the matter to form is unyielding to the effects of the mechanism into which it is put but the volume, mass and gravitational effects very much are. It is by influencing these variables that the thinking mechanism processors data (thinks) with the differing degrees of applied force being due to the data being input. More on this topic later.

So, this leaves us with the general question of what is happening at first level existence? We know from chapter four "Energy as a Single Dimension" in part three, that the form it takes is that of energy with no three dimensional extension. Three dimensional extensions are what first level existence looks like to us from our second level existence point of view. So to 'think' it must manipulate this single dimension of energy in some way.

This can't take the form of "moving it about" because it occupies no volume through which to move it. So the term "moving it about" is meaningless. This can only leave the manipulation of its energy levels throughout the entirety of its energy. By talking about manipulating energy levels throughout its entirety, you might suppose that would be impossible if it has no three dimensional extension (and therefore no entirety).

You might argue, very reasonably too, that if it has no three dimensional extension, it must occupy no space at all. What the particle physicist might otherwise refer to as a "point." Well this is quite so, but only from our second level existence point of view. This is how we see it while locked into our data processing activities within the mind of our Creator. We think in terms of three dimensions (four, to make density) because this is the way in which we process data: by living our every day lives through what we see and call four dimensions.

The whole argument could be stood on its head by saying that if this amount of energy, that constitutes our Creator, exists within no three dimensional constraints, then to say it exists in one point, with no such dimensional extensions, is placing just such a constraint upon it when in fact that constraint does not exist in first level existence. Come again?

If I have said that the energy in question has no volume (which I have), then from our second level existence point of view we can only conclude that it must be like a point. A point so small that it has no size. But to say that it is that "small" is to use the three dimensions of size. By using the term "small" we are unfairly placing a three dimensional constraint of size on it when in fact it exists in a form whereby the three dimensions of size are non-existent, because it is a single dimension called energy and no dimensions more.

Therefore, when I say that the single dimension, that goes to make our Creator, has no size, I mean precisely that: it has no size; size is not an issue, it is irrelevant, it is meaningless; there is no size attributable to it. To say it is small means nothing just as to say it is big or anything in between, means nothing. It simply exists as a single dimension. And as a single dimension of energy, it thinks, and in thinking it invokes our existence as data processing subunits that partly facilitates its thinking and by facilitating its thinking *we perceive* our day to day lives in what we understand as including the three dimensions of size (or volume).

Sorry to be "messing with your head" like this, as they put it. What I am asking you to envisage is outside of our normal experience. I am asking you to think one dimensionally, quite separately of the normal conventionally accepted three dimensions of volume and it takes some doing both in terms of understanding and explanation especially in view of the fact that I am forced to use four dimensional language to describe it and what's more, in light of what I am about to say.

If the single dimension of energy, in the first level of existence, has no volume, then from our point of view, in the second level of existence, any discrete quantity of that energy can be seen as being in every location at the same time. This is why, as explained in part three, when energy has rolled off the edge of our four dimensional universe to return to a single dimension again, it then manifests itself in each and every location at the same time within the universe to continue expanding into four dimensions again. This is an expansion that, when retarded, causes matter to form and the consequential gravitational effects that comes from that process. But that is from our point of view in the second level of existence. We are presently trying to view things from the first level of existence so as to get to the root cause of these differing rates of expansion. And to do that we need to understand how our Creator is manipulating its energy.

We have said it can't be due to moving it about because that infers volume. So, as we have also said, that can only leave the manipulation of energy level throughout its entirety and by entirety I do not mean its whole volume I mean the whole of its energy with no volume inferred.

Consciousness

From part three, chapter seven, "Why the Universe is Expanding and not Contracting or Static," I presented an expanding universe that was expanding in order to facilitate the thought processes of a Greater Intelligence. But that was a universe void of what we see as matter and it is the creation and interaction of matter that truly provides for its intricate thought processes. Therefore, what we had envisaged was only its *consciousness*, in the form of an expanding universe created from 'smooth' energy, void of matter, suitable for (although not actually) data processing. A suitability which is supported by continuous *consciousness* (continuous expansion).

This means that to achieve consciousness, it must simultaneously lower the energy level of all of the energy. This manifests itself, from our second level existence universe point of view, as appearing to be energy, continuously expanding to form a volumetric extension that we call the expanding universe.

159

The Ultimate Explanation

This would appear to be a rather grand assumption on my part. Why should it be that lowering its single dimensional energy level should equate to what appears to us as an expanding universe? I have in fact already answered this question in part three, chapter three, subheading "Energy as the prime mover". There we covered the topic of volumes and energy levels. We said that a good analogy of this would be to imagine a rectangle made of matches, first glued at their ends and then placed onto a sheet of rubber which is being stretched in all directions. The rubber was to represent the energy of an expanding universe. As it is stretched we could see that the rubber in the rectangle was continuously reducing in density (a location of reducing density). We then removed the matches and drew a square onto the rubber sheet and started it stretching again. The square was seen to grow but the amount of the rubber within that square always remained constant.

We therefore concluded that the universe has come into existence by virtue of all the locations within it being locations of increasing volume, expanding into an increasingly larger volume by virtue of every location within it being a location of reducing density. The reducing density in question is the density of energy. In other words, it is **REDUCING-ENERGY** which is the *prime mover* which *then* causes volume to exist in an ever expanding fashion. It is not the increase in volume that primarily drives it to expand - it is the ever reducing energy that constitutes that volume. Returning to the rubber sheet analogy, in the context of energy being the prime mover, it is not the sheet being stretched that causes it to expand but the effect of the density-of-rubber-per-unit-area reducing at every location within the sheet which THEN causes it to expand (with rubber representing energy). A bit like laying it on a hot plate and watching it melt into an expanded version of its former self, rather than trying to stretch it by hand.

160

So what I have said is that if the **ENERGY IS RE-DUCED** in each and every location, then the volume must expand especially given that the shape of the universe is such that it has no edge (resulting in the four dimensional roll) and as such has no form of confinement with which to prevent the expansion. Energy is the single dimension of the mind of our Creator and volume is the multidimensional appearance of our second level existence universe. It is simply an equation between single-dimensional pure intelligence and the multidimensional way in which it *appears* to us as part of that intelligence. Its just how we see things and the way in which we see things is as an expanding universe.

The manipulation of these energy levels, in such a way as to provide the simultaneous reduction of all the energy, (and thereby creating the expanding universe as perceived by us) is not something the Greater Intelligence *decides* to do. It is simply an *intrinsic* result of thinking as we shall see. Further, it does not need to continuously reduce its energy levels in order to produce a continuously expanding universe (and therefore its consciousness). To do so means it would eventually reduce to nothing and you can't reduce something to nothing when it's the only thing that exists. The fact is, it only needs to reduce the energy levels sufficiently to produce the four dimensional roll as described in part three, chapter three, "The Expanding Universe." After that the universe will appear to us as continuously expanding infinitum and thereby continuously providing a suitability for the Greater Intelligence's thought processes by bringing it into consciousness.

But, by the same principle, if the Greater Intelligence reduces *all* its energy levels by the same amount, albeit only sufficient to produce the four dimensional roll, then the amount by which that energy has reduced must have gone somewhere. But there is nowhere for it to go outside of the whole of the energy which, in itself, is all of existence. Thereby requiring that in fact only *some* of its energy has been reduced as a result of other energies having increased (see figure two on page 150). This must be so, as well we know; energy cannot be destroyed or created, only relocated. And by "relocated" I mean one energy level compared to another, in this single dimensional context. The Greater Intelligence only has a finite amount of energy with which to be conscious and think. This can only mean, as I have said, that some, and not all, of the energy has reduced. With the amount by which some of the energy has been reduced, going to provide increased energy levels 'elsewhere'.

Still looking at figure two, the reduced energy levels therefore explains what appears to us as expanding (so called - empty) space (consciousness of the Greater Intelligence) that constitutes the expanding universe but how do these energy levels, that have correspondingly increased, figure in the scheme of things?

Thinking

The answer is quite simple. The energy has gone to create what we see as matter. Put in second level existence terms (which is how we see it in the "ultimate model of the universe" - see figure one on page 12); the concentration, or increase, of energy into a three dimensional region of space. That is; an increased level of energy when measured relative to the lower concentration of surrounding space, with space and energy being one and the same, as explained in part two. This matter, as said before, is what provides the intricate thinking process of the Greater Intelligence.

The problem here is one of trying to picture such a first level existence process. We can't. We can only think in four dimensions at best (in our second level of existence) and what we are trying to picture is one dimensional with no three dimensional extension. So, to think of it in four dimensional terms is the only interpretation we can place on it, given that our minds are locked in the four dimensional second level existence universe. So the best way I can do that is to free myself of trying to talk one dimensionally and invoke a model that is four dimensional but that should be taken as inferring the one dimension of energy. One such model is our old friend the sponge model.

Like that, if the overall size of the sponge were to represent the overall energy level of the Greater Intelligence, that energy level would be seen to reduce when the red spherical areas condensed within it. In just the same way as the spherical wall of the overall sponge would follow inwards as the spheres condensed. The two condensing spheres are to represent two increases in energy level within in the mind of the Greater Intelligence. By their increase, the overall energy level of the Greater Intelligence reduces in the same way that the overall sponge size gets smaller. That is, all of the energy level, considered separately of the two increased levels, would have correspondingly dropped when compared to that of the two increased energy levels.

Again looking at figure two, this reduction in what *appears* to be *all* of the Greater Intelligence's energy level (by the overall sponge shape reducing in size), presents itself as the cause of the second level existence universe to expand into a four dimensional roll. This is what we presently call the expanding universe, or rather; the expanding space between lumps of matter.

Utilising the sponge analogy further, every area of increased energy, within the sponge (single dimensional mind of the Greater Intelligence) is what we perceive as a particle of matter in our second level existence multidimensional universe. The varying degrees of energy level represent the different attributes of that matter in the form of different rates of expanding energy in our universe, which appears to us as areas of increased energy, forming matter.

163

This is the frame work for the thinking process, with the interaction of matter, and everything that it forms at our second level existence universe, being the actual thinking process as witnessed by our minds in the form of data processing sub-units (processing data by the act of being intelligent).

So, to return to the concept of consciousness and thinking: it is the interaction of this matter that constitutes the thinking process of the Greater Intelligence. A thinking process which is facilitated by its consciousness (the expanding universe), which itself is brought about by the act of creating matter with which to think.

To make clear: consciousness and thinking are not two separate things. To think is to be conscious and to be conscious is to think. But, for the purpose of explaining the expanding universe and its cause in part three, it best served my ends to have presented the two as being separate, with consciousness being the expansion of 'smooth' energy into a four dimensional universe, void of matter, which is under going a four dimensional roll as a result of that expansion. But it is by now considering the true nature of "The mind of our Creator," in this chapter that we realise that it is matter that provides the intricate thinking process and that the two have to be brought together to realise that the expansion of the universe is by virtue of the matter created within it. When the Greater Intelligence thinks, the universe rolls; queue for a song I think!

When considering the consequences as they make themselves obvious in the second level of existence universe, the intrinsic effect of the Greater Intelligence causing changes in its own energy levels to provide its thinking process, is the effect of the **Primary Force of Expansion** (figure two on page 150). That is, in the form of different rates of expansion, with the primary force of expansion providing the substratum of expanding space in which matter sits. Matter is being formed by the effect of higher energy levels (in the mind of our Creator), manifesting themselves as a slower rate of expansion in our universe which then appear to us as particles of matter. These areas of slower-rate expanding energy are caused by the **Retarded Primary Force of Expansion**.

It should be noted that the Primary Force of Expansion and the Retarded Primary Force of Expansion are only arbitrary names. They could just as easily be called "high force of pink elephants" and "low force of pink elephants," it makes little difference. The important thing to grasp is the meaning they impart: that when, within the mind of the Greater Intelligence, different levels of energy are adjusted to provide for its thought, these manifest themselves as different rates of expanding space/energy (one and the same) within our universe (also its thinking mechanism - or mind). This is then, according to conventional thinking, what we see as different densities of space/energy. Different *densities* and not *different rates-of-expansion* because we don't realise that we, and everything else in the entire universe, is expanding (other than to realise that so called empty space is expanding).

Summary

Despite my recent reference to pink elephants, I will add that I deliberately use the word "force" when describing the cause of expansion, particularly in the case of the retarded primary force of expansion. In that instance, as I have said before, **the force is unyielding but the volume, that each degree of force produces, is variable and results in different densities and mass under the influence of the surroundings in which each body of mass finds itself** i.e. the influence of other gravitational fields[1]. This has to be the

[1]   *The force remains constant but the retarded rate of expansion of the energy that it is controlling varies in accordance with its surroundings.*

case. As I have said before: the Greater Intelligence inputs the data by the formation of matter under the influence of its force. The mass/volume/density that the matter then takes on and the way in which it interacts with other lumps of matter, all of which are formed in this way, is then the data processing activity of its mind. It is at the will of the data processing mechanism that we see as, and call "the universe."

The primary force of expansion is a slightly different kettle of fish. As explained earlier, the primary cause of expansion is the force that causes the expansion of so called empty space to the point that the outer most extension goes through zero density, causing the constituent energy to continuously roll in on itself in the form of, what I have called; a four dimensional roll. This is effectively "consciousness" and is as a direct result of matter forming and the formation of matter is the process of the Creator inputting data. Once formed, that matter is then influenced by the natural will of the thinking mechanism into which it is input; what we call "the universe" which is processing data under the name of "thinking" in order to provide an output. (You might remember: "when the Creator thinks the universe rolls!").

This is all in second level existence terms and exactly transposes across from the single dimension of energy doing its thing by way of manipulating energy levels as an intrinsic result of thinking, which is intelligence, which is energy. (See figure two on page 150). A discrete quantity (no volume inferred) of increased energy level within the entirety of energy = retarded primary force of expansion = slower expanding energy (slower compared to the result of the primary force of expansion) = the formation of a discrete quantity (volume *is* inferred) of matter.

Still looking at figure two, if matter is the result of an increase in energy level within the mind of our Creator, then that increase in energy must cause a reduction in energy level elsewhere (no volume inferred) and the 'elsewhere' from which it is removed is the reduced energy level that causes space to expand. This space (energy) is low level energy that we see as expanding space between matter which is low level energy that we measure as not being matter and therefore we call it empty! (see also page 116). So we can see that this low level energy (as a result of matter forming) = the primary force of expansion = faster expanding energy/space (faster compared to the result of the retarded force) = expanding space between matter, or as is the same thing: the substratum of space in which matter sits.

The very important subtlety to be appreciated through all of this is that the primary force of expansion is a reaction to the retarded primary force of expansion. The more retarded-areas-of-expanding-energy that form (matter), the more space expands (expands faster). Likewise, the more that any existing retarded areas are retarded, the more space expands (expands faster).

The retarded force is the input of the Creator and as such it is unyielding; it is constant; it represents the nature of that input of data to the system and if it varied willy-nilly then the data would be corrupted. The primary force reacts and tugs back on that area so as to try and expand it at the same rate as itself and a field of gravity is set up from the resulting tug-of-war between the forces. When another retarded area forms by way of input to the system, the primary force reacts all the more. Its increased reaction is felt by the other existing retarded areas whose volumes increase as a result even though the retarded force, that formed those volumes in the first place, remains constant. This set up is one that I described in "The Non-Expanding Ultimate Model" in part four, chapter five, (especially under the subheading "Universal forces") which transposes across to the expanding version.

The volume, that a retarded primary force of expansion causes to form (no retardation of expansion = no discernible volume), changes all sorts of variables within the thinking mechanism as we have seen before. Mass/matter/density (all the same thing) and gravity are influenced by volume, which constitutes a disturbance which is transmitted throughout the entire system because it is closed. This is the intrinsic process of the Creator (Greater Intelligence) thinking.

So it can be seen that the primary force is variable according to circumstances, and the retarded force is constant according to the nature of the data being input.

So what is the Greater Intelligence thinking about?

All of existence is not one single lump of intelligence. It is certainly a single entity that is our Creator but it is one that is composed of many individual intelligences within the whole that forms layers and sub-layers of intelligences, all exchanging data. After all; you can't buy a packet of sweets without speaking to the shop keeper. If it were a single lump of intelligence it would have nowhere to deliver its outputs and nowhere from which to receive inputs. It would have nothing to think about and be rendered 'brain dead'. We would disappear like a puff of logical smoke.

The nature of these levels of intelligence, how we figure within them and a journey through them will be the subject of book four which will address the many questions that arise from the above including the exact nature of the output of data. For now we have the general "base case" of what is going on in relation to the universe that we perceive as surrounding us, which is the intention of this first book. The reason I am making the point here; that the Greater Intelligence is composed of individual intelligences, is to try and defuse the question "well what is he thinking about?" until book four. The fact is, it doesn't think like you and I. It *is* by *virtue* of you and I, and by virtue of everything that comprises all of creation. And all of creation follows rational and logical rules; a cosmos. Therefore it is a rational logical system of intelligence (energy) and another word for the act of carrying out intelligence is to "think." It is as intelligent as all of the layers of intelligences from which it is formed with humans forming only one layer. This makes it so much more intelligent then we are that the comparison is beyond words. It knows and influences all we feel, do, and strive for, and infinitely beyond. It reckons from one moment to the next with all the degrees and manifestations of happiness, love/hate that acts as the prime mover behind human society, as well as all the activities throughout all the universe.

Believe me, its intelligence is so vast that to consider that it might ponder the question of having its eggs fried or boiled, would be pathetic beyond comprehension. Humans don't have a monopoly of the word "think" just because that is what we do with *our* minds at *our* level of intelligence. It is indeed the case that what we do *is* intelligent (because what we do is an act of intelligence) but there is still much that is vastly more intelligent for which the term "think" can be equally applied.

What it thinks about is all that goes on within all of creation, and *that* goes beyond the four dimensions that *we think of* as the 'physical' universe. What it thinks about influences all of creation and all of creation influences *it* - they are one and the same. The answer cannot be plainer. The question is; what goes on in all of creation? that we might then understand the answer.

The output

Just as I have touched upon the question of what the Greater Intelligence is thinking about, in advance of book four, it seems a pity to have come this far and not, at least, touch upon the output mechanism in the system I have so far described, even though it is also outside the scope of this book. Especially as the answer puts human beings back at the intellectual centre of the universe. But I am loathed to give too many details because it requires some considerable justification, which is the job of book four. But in a nut shell; we are very much part of that output. In effect, we are the eyes and ears of the Greater Intelligence.

If we are mini images of the Greater Intelligence, intrinsically designed to process data as part of the Greater Intelligence, we are far from helpless puppets on the end of strings. Certainly we are here at its will; to do its bidding, but we are also *part* of its will *and* its bidding. We help to create it and influence it at our level of intelligence. This is why we must look to ourselves as prime drivers of the cold common sense logic that we call good and evil. A logic that I shall examine in book four. But for now, those that might feel offended at the prospect of being nothing more than a glorified calculator might start to see how it is that we are every bit as clever as we think we are. Each and everyone of us is crucial to the drive of all creation to sustain intelligence. The thought of a human intelligence simply shuffling off the end of its mortal coil to never again figure in the equation of all creation in all its eternal glory, is nothing short of simplistic and caveman like. It defeats logic. Just as something cannot pop out from nothing, so too something cannot pop back in. Besides, there is no such thing as nothing!

CHAPTER 2
THE ROLLING PIN OF ACADEMIC CRUCIFIXION

The constraint of fluidity

Previously we have looked at the first level existence and second level existence formation of matter. Matter which is energy that is expanding with a retarded rate of expansion which then appears to the rest of the faster expanding energy (space) as if it has contracted. This is an *apparent* contraction that causes the surrounding energy (space) to take on an a *change in* density which follows an inverse square law with respect to distance from the centre of matter, which is what we call a gravitational field - see figure two on page 150. (Remembering that "change in" means the density compared to that which prevailed before the matter formed). This field then attracts other formations of matter.

All very well but I made the point earlier, under the subheading "Tank Model," in part four, chapter four (which was designed to be a non-expanding mimic of the expanding universe at large), that a four dimensional system with condensed matter in it would *not* provide for an attraction between two condensed bodies of matter. This was because it is a fluid system in which the energy that would otherwise be responsible for drawing them together, by increasing in density, would simply shuffle about to provide an unchanged uniform density throughout the rest of the system that would leave no net attraction between the condensed bodies of matter. The question then has to be asked: how then does the expanding version of the same thing over come this problem? Or rather; how does the expanding, apparently fluid, universe behave like a non-fluid when it comes to the propagation of gravity?

First I will quickly recap on what I mean by fluid in this context. We can say that the universe behaves as though it is fluid because the bodies of matter within it, attract each other under the force of gravity in such a way as to draw together, from whatever three dimensional angle, to the point that they are capable of making surface to surface contact. This is much like the bubble model that had this fluid property on its two dimensional surface. In the case of the universe, this then is three dimensional movement on the part of the constituent lumps of matter that can be described as being fluid. "Fluid" because they are all free to move to whatever extent at whatever angle they like in a system of which they form part. So it seems logical to think that the universe is a fluid system.

But! quite apart from the fluid property that lumps of matter can boast by way of their movement, as soon as we afford the rest of the system (so called empty space), the same fluid characteristic, we find that the gravitational attraction, between the lumps of matter, falls to bits. This is because the energy, that forms the 'empty space,' is also able to move about to any full three dimensional extent if it too is to be regarded as fluid. So when the gravity, exhibited by two lumps of matter, tries to increase the density of energy between them, which would otherwise pull them together, the empty-space-energy simply shuffles about to leave no such increase in density that would pull them together (see subheading "Tank model," part four, chapter four).

So the universe is clearly not fluid in all respects. With respect to the movement of matter; yes. With respect to the behaviour of the energy that forms 'empty space;' no. This is why I have referred to the universe as *apparently* fluid. This is also where we had to cheat to describe gravity in the universe in the foregoing chapters; by saying it is only fluid in certain respects. I have therefore set myself a constraint - The constraint of fluidity.

The rolling pin of constraints

The reader will undoubtedly be aware by now that the whole book has rolled forward as driven by constraints and the constraint of fluidity is no exception. It is by providing the key to unlock one constraint after the next that we have continuously moved closer to the overall picture. But the constraint of fluidity is a rather special one. It is of course a constraint that I must hope to remedy in order to sustain a unified theory and believe me I can. The answer lies firmly in the fact that the universe is expanding. It requires no reliance on the Greater Intelligence, it is simple and straight forward and what's more, is intrinsic in what I have already said in this book. But, as you've guessed with this run-up, I am not about to "let on." It forms the first issue in book two. A cop out? No. The reason is as follows:-

This book is intended to provide the basic principles of the macroscopic universe: its "big" aspects. What it is, what its up to, how it generally works. To do this I have unwittingly presented a case that quite often flies in the face of convention. I say unwittingly because I didn't set out by saying "right, what does convention say, let's come up with something contrary or bend convention to fit." I simply had a vision of the overall scheme of things that doesn't always run with current thinking. I didn't even consider convention until I occasionally took a side ways glance to see what convention had to say.

The result is that I have found myself with a rolling pin in my hand, running it over the unshaped dough of reality to provide the start of a unified explanation. But in doing so I have unavoidably thrown up constraints in front of it, some of which I have set myself and some set by convention. These are constraints that have been ironed out with successive rolls of the pin as we have moved through the book, only to throw up more. This is healthy, and as it should be, but as soon as I lift the pin, every man and his academic dog will hit me over the head with it declaring that I've left a problem that is insurmountable and against which a unified theory falls.

Well, soon I shall have to lift it as I come to the end of this first book. And yes, I will leave constraints to be ironed out in book two. Certainly hold it aloft but reserve your strike until book two. The constraints I will be starting with are as I have set myself, as follows:-

Firstly; the boundary constraint. How can the universe have expanded to the point of rolling in on itself when first it must have got there with an expanding front. A front that requires a boundary formed by nothing when nothing does not exist! I reserve the answer until book two because it gives us an explanation which is analogous of the big bang theory. It will also describe the beginning of the universe and what came before. And what's more, like the Big Bang theory, it will also detail how, what we call the "microwave background radiation" comes about, which is "electromagnetic radiation" which, as I will explain, is movement and movement forms the scope of the next book. This background radiation issue is fundamental to the argument and so the whole 'shooting match' must fall off the edge of this book and into the next.

Put another way, if I explained one small part that gave a clue to many others, I could conceivably encourage a glorified "second guessing" exercise that would pre-empt the other books. This is in stark contrast to having the concepts I have already revealed, nailed to the academic cross. I walk a thin tightrope from which it is best to sectionalise the release of the theory in order to keep it "single sourced," although there is still scope for second guessing even now.

And so it is with the second constraint; the constraint of fluidity. To me this is a beautiful constraint because it gives us the speed at which the universe is expanding, the answer to what inertia is and most exiting of all, the true nature of light. But light and inertia, along with electromagnetic radiation, are movement and so they fall into the scope of the next book. I could not even start the justification and logic behind the answer to either constraint without describing light and inertia, so into the next book these constraints must fall. They fall into a pot along with time because, as I have already said many times, time is movement and *appears* dimensional because that movement warps three dimensionally.

That is not to suggest that these are the only questions that arise from the theory so far. Far from it. But if I spent every section trying to address every particle of academic crucifixion that might come my way, I would never impart the general frame work of the beginnings of a holistic theory. But as a holistic theory, the other books will repeatedly address topics we have already covered with a second roll of the pin, and a third, and a fourth, and so on. The dough is circular and will become thinner and clearer with each roll.

The ether and entropy

An example of the questions that arise so far is the very controversial subject of the ether. I have said it exists in the form of expanding low level energy. The reason the Michelson Morley experiment (and others of its kind) failed to detect it lies in the answer to the fluidity constraint and so will be explained and answered in book two. The true nature of light also plays a big part in answering this question.

Then there is the subject of **entropy**. That too will be answered along with the question of the ether in book two. Not to mention the catalogue of questions that will eventually be addressed in all the other books. One thing at a time.

The unification between steady state and expanding universe

But there is one topic of movement that can be brought quite neatly into this book and that is the subject of the steady state universe. For those that might not know, the idea of a universe that is expanding is not one that everyone agrees with. There are still those that believe it is steady state. That is, not expanding but simply there. In a state that only three dimensional movement takes place on the part of the matter that makes up the universe without continuously rushing away from each other. Einstein himself believed this but later came to regret it. His belief is what gave rise to his "cosmological constant."

But by looking at what I have already said, it becomes obvious that the universe is both.

Briefly, the rationale behind this is as follows. If you place a ruler between, say; two clusters of galaxies, to measure the distance between them, given that I am suggesting that not only is space expanding but everything in it, as the space between the clusters expands, so too does the ruler and the clusters. So, from one cluster to the other, each would not appear to move away, they would still look to be the same size and the ruler would still show the same distance. Yet light would be red-shifted because the clusters, in absolute terms, are rushing away from each other, giving the occupants of the clusters the *impression* that they are moving apart. Although, it has to be said, if the clusters (or any astronomical body for that matter) are moving three dimensionally with respect to one another, they would of course appear, from one to the other, to be doing just that. (No continual creation of matter is necessary, as proposed by Fred Hoyle and Co.'s Steady State Theory in 1948).

It can be genuinely said that the distance between the clusters is not increasing even though they are rushing apart. If this seems nonsensical it is only because we need to examine what is meant by "distance." The fact is that the only thing by which we gauge the existence of distance (or "displacement" if you prefer) is the equipment that we use to measure it and if that tells us that the distance is not increasing then it must be true, just as to say that the universe is physical is true; because that is what we care to call it. It is simply the case that definition causes complication, not reality. The reality is that they are rushing apart and expanding in the process.

Black holes

There is also much I have not mentioned that I could have done, things that I shall cover subsequently, like black holes for instance - there is no need for singularities and infinities that play havoc with the mathematics of Relativity (not to mention common-sense). Infinite densities and zero volumes need not occupy the centres of collapsed stars. Black holes are simply due to the behaviour of an extremely retarded rate of expansion, the centre of which is continuously expanding with as much volume and density as fits comfortably and logically within any reasoning mind.

The subject of a singularity at the beginning of the universe (the Big Bang) requires a subtle rotation of the "apparent need for one" to be viewed from a more enlightening angle to reveal what happened at the beginning and before. I hope to see you in book two for that, along with more on black holes.

CHAPTER 3
CLOSING THE LOOP

Finally, this is an holistic theory and as such you may often consider any one argument as weak or fantastic, or both. But, by progressing through it regardless, each element serves to endorse the others. If I could deliver the entire thing in one parallel lump of information, I would, with the whole bearing out the whole in one swift exercise. But I can't. I am bound within the walls of serial behaviour and thereby limited to delivery in serialised discrete packages of information, in this case, in the form of one page after the other, and one book after the other. But this last part of the book serves as an example of bolstering other parts by portraying the true function of the conventionally accepted three dimensions as I am about to explain. (We are now ready to start closing the loop):-

In part one I said that existence is pure intelligence. In part two I said that the three conventionally accepted dimensions can be reduced to one, that of volume. In part three I made the case that energy is the forth dimension, and the *only* dimension, that can be *academically* divided into four to describe density. I also said that energy is what constructs these four dimensions into density by the act of expanding into a volume. In parts four and five I have shown that this volume (three dimensions) is what facilitates intelligence by the formation of matter in an apparently three dimensional thinking mechanism that we call the universe. This shows that the three dimensions are the *act* of intelligence (processing data). Intelligence is pure unadulterated energy which is a single dimension that constructs the other three by being intelligent. This leads us right back to the first part of the book which sets about describing existence as pure intelligence.

This is a circle and one that I shall make larger and clearer through the other books in this series but as a circle, to start an explanation of it is difficult. For a circle has no start or finish and to jump on at any point is to invoke the incredible straight away simply because the rest has not been journeyed in order to make that arbitrary start point a credible one. This is why I asked at the start of this book that the idea of existence, in the form that I was offering it, should only be taken as a suggestion, albeit an incredible suggestion. Its justification lay ahead throughout the remainder of the book and still begs more by way of the remainder in this series. This I shall provide.

Blasphemy against convention

At the end of the day,
when all is said and done.
When day's long strife is complete,
and light withdraws with the evening sun.

To make all things fair,
your pride at ease,
reflect on what has gone before.
Know yourself - and please.

Please your nature,
soothe your furrowed brow.
Draw upon that inner strength,
as only you know how.

For, to have stood against the opinion of others,
swallowed hard against their bitter, spiteful pleasure,
is to count small gains against their will,
as gleaming items of treasure.

Treasure that stands out proud and profound,
but do the gems of convention dwindle in surround?
No - not any one is wrong or conventionally correct,
simply all stacked together, for the human mind to collect.

———

DETAILED CONTENTS